THE SOLDIER WHO
CAME BACK

STEVE FOSTER
and ALAN CLARK

Mirror Books

Published by Mirror Books,
an imprint of Trinity Mirror plc,
1 Canada Square,
London E14 5AP, England

www.mirrorbooks.co.uk

ISBN 9781907324239

First hardback edition

Every effort has been made to fulfil requirements with regard to
reproducing copyright material. The author and publisher will be
glad to rectify any omissions at the earliest opportunity.

Front cover images: Getty Images, iStockphoto

Typeset by Danny Lyle

DanJLyle@gmail.com

This book is dedicated to Staff Sergeant Thomas Aitken,
Royal Army Ordnance Corps who, with selfless bravery,
fought hard against the dreadful conditions faced by his
fellow soldiers on the Forced March of 1945.

CONTENTS

Prologue   1

PART ONE
ANTONY AND FRED
Chapter One   9
Chapter Two   23
Chapter Three   38
Chapter Four   50
Chapter Five   61
Chapter Six   74

PART TWO
THE ESCAPE
Chapter Seven   85
Chapter Eight   111
Chapter Nine   130
Chapter Ten   147

PART THREE
LOST AND FOUND
Chapter Eleven   157
Chapter Twelve   172
Chapter Thirteen   188

Postscript   207

PROLOGUE

It slept peacefully in a corner, squashed in among the usual stuff that we abandon in our attics. Cardboard boxes sagging with unwanted books. The sad tennis racket with the broken string. Your auntie's hideous antique clock that might be worth something if you can ever be bothered to find out.

It was a simple old suitcase; small, dull, utilitarian. Made of some drab grey material, its locks were now rusty and coming away from the structure. It had definitely belonged to a man. The interior revealed no frills or flounces, no luxurious lining of watered silk. No woman would ever entrust it with her cashmeres, her kid gloves or her satin dress. This suitcase was as far from Louis Vuitton as it was possible to get. It was an object born of harder, leaner times, given to my father when he was demobbed after World War Two. Inside it, though I did not discover this for many years, was his life. It was only when I finally opened it that I would really get to know him.

It is a truth universally acknowledged that a man who has just retired must be in search of an occupation. And so it was with me. After half a lifetime at sea, I suddenly found myself high and dry, beached in a village near Winchester. I had been an engineer officer in The Royal Navy, but the only thing I was in charge of now was cutting the lawn, walking the dogs and making sure we got a parking space at Sainsbury's. My pride and joy was my motorcycle, which I cared for as if it were a particularly delicate child, but there is only so much time you can spend tearing along the leafy lanes of Hampshire in the driving rain. Increasingly, I was getting under my wife's feet; any day now, she'd sweep me into her dustpan and brush. The charms of the bowling green held no allure. Every morning I felt like an artist contemplating an empty canvas with no idea what to paint. Like many newly retired men, I was finding the transition difficult. Something had to be done.

The new popularity of TV programmes on genealogy drew me towards the notion of researching my family tree. The internet age meant it had never been easier to go digging into your past and find out exactly who you were. Genealogy is the perfect pastime for later life. When you're young, you're too excited about the present and future to give a damn about the past. It's only when you become uncomfortably aware of your own mortality that you start to want to know. It is, quite literally, a case of now or never.

I set about it dutifully, sitting at my computer in the small bedroom I'd turned into a study, as the dogs romped in the back garden and my wife cheerfully set about her vacuuming with no useless hulk getting in the way.

I realised I was setting out on some sort of journey. What I didn't realise was that it would be a journey that would both change and illuminate my life. But there would be a paradox involved. Because in one sense I didn't get very far, whilst, in another, I got further than I could have imagined possible.

At the start of the process, I followed the usual route into the genealogical maze, joining various websites, convinced I'd soon discover that my unknown ancestors included some famous highwayman, celebrated wit, or a sailor who had stood beside Nelson at Trafalgar. Perhaps I might be descended from a duke, even if on the wrong side of the blanket.

'Don't forget Dad's old suitcase,' said my sister casually one day. 'There must be some good stuff in there.'

Fred Foster, my father, had died twenty years before in 1990. My mother not long afterwards. Before she passed away, she, too, had told me to remember the suitcase. It seemed important, as if it represented some part of him that remained to her.

After her death, I and my sister had faithfully opened it, but after a cursory glance at some of its contents, had soon closed it again. The loss of our parents was still too recent, the wounds still too raw. And so the suitcase stayed in dusty darkness. It wasn't until 2010, when I began my journey into the family history, that I finally braved the attic, brushed off the cobwebs and carried it downstairs into the light. It was to be a revelation.

Inside were things I had expected to find. The usual family pictures, black and white or fading now to yellow: my parents as babes in arms; my sister and I snapped at the Lincolnshire seaside, ice-cream cones in happy hands. There were certificates of my father's various professional qualifications. Letters of congratulation and praise when, in his prime, he had become a prominent man. There were other letters, too, between my father and mother, but I soon found these too private and personal, even so long after their deaths. The correspondence was mostly from the war years; a time when people tried to say exactly what they felt in case they never got the chance to do so again. Every word straight from the heart.

Fred Foster rarely spoke about the war, at least not to his children. If he did, it was usually in generalities, rather than his own experience. I knew he'd served in Norway, been captured and held prisoner in Poland, but that was pretty much it. Every year, he got on the train to London for an annual reunion with his surviving mates and returned the next day with a sore head. Now and again, one or other of these 'old codgers' came to stay for a day or two. But like most young people, I was so wrapped up in my own life that I hardly bothered to ask. I grew up in the Sixties; Mods and Rockers, Jimi Hendrix and Eric Clapton, flower power, give peace a chance and all that jazz. World War Two belonged to a distant age, as remote as The Crusades or Henry V at Agincourt. So there were no touching scenes where we sat together by the fireside, father and son, as he shared those events that had, in so many ways, made him the man he had eventually become.

But two decades after his passing, that omission was to be rectified. From beyond the grave, my father finally spoke. In the depths of the geriatric suitcase, I was to discover, like some lost jewel, a story. It gripped me in an instant and has never since let me go. A chronicle of courage, selflessness and sacrifice, which seemed to me to be one of the most remarkable and exciting of World War Two. At once, I forgot about delving further back into my family history. I would never discover if I was the illegitimate descendant of a duke. Here instead was the tale that deserved to be told.

In its essence, it was about two young men who formed an unlikely friendship. An alliance of guts, daring and, sometimes, sheer bloody recklessness in order to stick four fingers up at the monstrousness of the Third Reich. One of these men was my father Fred Foster. The other was called Antony Coulthard.

But I knew at once there was something more to this story. It wasn't just a fascinating relic of a long-gone time, like all those yellowing photographs. This was a tale that wasn't yet finished because, above it, like a dark, unmoving cloud, hung one big question mark. It was a question that, I now believe, also hung heavily in my father's heart till the day he died. Until the answer to that question was found, the ending could never be written. So I set myself the task of finding it. And if I could succeed in doing so, I could also repay a debt from one man to another that had been owed for all these years.

This book tells the story in the suitcase. Its beginning, its middle and now, at last, its end.

PART ONE

ANTONY AND FRED

CHAPTER ONE

For a bricklayer, Harry Foster possessed sadly few bricks of his own. His home at 32 Bowbridge Road in Newark was a tiny dwelling in a dusty terrace of identical houses, each no more than fifteen feet wide, as if the working classes must be squashed tightly together to take up as little space as possible.

Newark itself was a nice enough town, reasonably prosperous, set on the Great North Road in the flatlands of Nottinghamshire. It boasted a wide market square lined with historic buildings, a majestic church and the ruins of a great Norman castle towering above the River Trent. But in the early years of the twentieth century, Bowbridge Road was a mean street on the wrong side of the tracks. Like its neighbours, Number 32 had no front door but was entered from the rear, via a communal passageway leading from the street. Inside there was no proper lobby or hall, just two small rooms with an interconnecting door. Off the back room, which had a fireplace, was a lean-to construction that housed a narrow scullery with an old white enamel sink. The sink had only one cold tap. Water for cleaning and washing had to be boiled in a kettle. A steep staircase led up to two poky bedrooms. The loo was outside in the backyard. Like the rest of the house, it was dark, dingy and cramped.

The only saving grace was that this was a house with love in it. Harry the bricklayer had married a fine girl called Ethel and soon they had two children: my father Fred was born in 1915 and his sister Hilda not long after. But Harry and Ethel were chalk and cheese; a man of little ambition and a woman who longed for a better life. Bricklaying was the Foster family trade. Harry's father and two brothers were 'brickies', too. Harry laboured hard all week and, on a Friday night, gave Ethel what she needed for the housekeeping then spent the rest in the pub where he drank as hard as he worked. Harry cheerfully accepted this as his lot in life. If it had been good enough for his father, it was good enough for him. He was not ashamed of the brick-dust under his fingernails.

But Ethel was different. She had drive and energy. She knew there was another world beyond Bowbridge Road and wanted her children to discover it. Her Fred was not to be weighed down by a brickie's hod and a dead-end existence. He and Hilda could and must do better. But all of Ethel's dreams were soon to be blotted out when she developed a brain tumour and died at the age of thirty-nine, when Fred was only twelve and Hilda ten. She had given them her complete devotion and they had returned it. They were devastated.

So, of course, was Harry. He had stood at Ethel's graveside wondering how on earth he was going to raise them without a mother. The answer soon became all too clear. He couldn't. He found it impossible to cope. For a while he drowned his desolation in a beer mug, then set out to find a new wife. His gaze alighted on a widow with a young son, the same age as Fred. It was a disastrous choice. Underneath the wedding veil of Harry's blushing bride was a 'wicked' stepmother just waiting to get out. As in a fairytale, the children of the first wife were demeaned and persecuted. She gave her own son bacon and eggs while her husband's children got bread and dripping. All of Ethel's light and love had vanished from 32 Bowbridge Road and misery had replaced it.

But some years later, there would be a happy, if bizarre, ending. One day, Harry and his children came home to find the house strangely empty. Not only had the wicked stepmother and her spoilt son disappeared, most of the furniture had, too. It was a midday flit. They vanished into thin air and were never seen or heard of ever again. No attempt was made to find them, although Harry remained married to her till the day he died.

Through all of this, young Fred Foster had watched and waited. He loved his father; Harry was a good man after all. But, as he grew, Fred could see him in a clearer light, could see what Harry's lassitude and lack of purpose had condemned him to. By now, two of Harry's brick-laying brothers had started a building business of their own and had offered Harry a role in the enterprise. But Harry had declined. He had no urge to build anything more. He sat in the dingy back parlour in his shirtsleeves, wreathed in the pungent smoke of Woodbines, till the day the undertaker came to carry him out of it.

What Fred loved much more, however, was the memory of Ethel. She had nourished him with the notion that, if he tried hard enough, there was almost nothing he couldn't do, nothing he couldn't be. For the rest of his life, the spirit of Ethel would be the wind beneath his wings. Above all, he was determined he would not become another Harry.

This, though, was easier said than done. The working-class children of Bowbridge Road all left school at fourteen. Grammar school was not for the likes of them, university an impossible dream. So, like all the lads he knew, young Fred walked out of the gates of the Mount School for the last time without an exam result to his name. It seemed that the brickie's hod might claim him after all.

But his natural intelligence had been noted by his teachers. With their good words behind him, he landed a job as a clerk in the office of a local builder and then, having quickly justified his teachers' faith in him, stepped onto the next rung as an articled clerk with a Newark solicitor. He would stay with Colton & Franks in Lombard Street for the next ten years, learning his trade and a lot more besides. In the stiff-collared, respectable office of a provincial law practice, the teenage Fred began to encounter the grown-up world, warts and all. In the daily parade of wills and testaments, of contracts and conveyancing, of crime and punishment, he was learning about the foibles, the follies and the fantasies that human flesh is heir to. The old cliché about the 'university of life' was never more true than in the case of Fred Foster.

It was here, too, he started to meet, and to deal with, educated people from different backgrounds to his own. He began to get glimpses of those wider horizons that Ethel had encouraged him to seek out and to see that he could be part of it if he strove to. And he did. He studied for certificates in subjects such as shorthand and typing. Every small success was another rung upwards. A chance was all he asked for.

Beyond hard work and a drive to succeed, Fred had another advantage. Nearly everybody liked him. Though not conventionally handsome, at over six feet tall he had presence. And he was warm, approachable, outgoing. The sort of bloke you'd enjoy having a drink with or chatting to on a train. Neither the humble circumstances of his upbringing nor the brevity of his education had made him in any way timid or reserved. Nor did he ever try to conceal his disadvantaged roots or to lose the East Midlands accent of his birth. He loved company and conversation, especially with those from whom he thought he could learn something. Fred was a young man who reached out to people with a sunny smile and a firm handshake, and people would reply in kind.

When he wasn't working or studying, Fred did the usual things that young men did. He drank in the pub with his mates. He took girls to see Clark Gable and Humphrey Bogart, The Marx Brothers, Fred Astaire and Ginger Rogers. Fred liked girls and girls liked Fred, but there was little chance of anything more than a smooch in the back row at the pictures or outside her house, keeping watch for her mum or dad peeking out from behind the net curtains.

In the 1930s, Newark felt the effects of The Depression. Though not as badly affected as the north of England, the East Midlands did not escape unscathed. The Jarrow Marchers, on their historic trek to London to demand action from the government on poverty and unemployment, passed through Nottingham, only twenty miles away, fed, watered and cheered on by the townsfolk. Luckily for Fred Foster, the machinery of the state would always require lawyers to make it run. So he was safe, protected from the worst of the hurricane by the sturdy brick walls of Colton & Franks. But that safety was not to last for long.

Chapter One

As Fred had grown towards adulthood, there was a parallel cloud that hung over the young people of his generation. In a couple of years, it would come to threaten everything they knew and all that they might hope for in the future. For the moment, the cloud seemed small enough and everybody still hoped for the best. Hitler was a cartoon character, they thought. Surely the Germans would soon get shot of this ranting fool? At the picture-house, they had all roared at Charlie Chaplin's impersonation in *The Great Dictator*. Anyway, the last war had only happened twenty years before; surely nobody would risk another? That nice but dull Mr Chamberlain would sort it all out.

Like many others, Fred Foster wasn't yet fearful of what was happening in Europe. After all, wasn't Thomas Cook, the travel company, still producing glossy brochures telling the British what a warm welcome awaited them on the continent and especially in Germany? In 1937, having saved enough money from his wages to make his first trip abroad, Fred went with a friend on a biking holiday to Luxembourg. As usual, he made new friends, flirted with girls and drank plenty of beer. In the pretty old town of Ettelbruck, with its winding cobbled streets and fairy-tale buildings, it was so easy to convince yourself the worst would never happen, that the peace of Europe wasn't splintering apart like a rotting barrel.

The following year, nice Mr Chamberlain flew to Munich to see Hitler and came back promising 'peace for our time'. It was so much more comfortable to believe in him than listen to the Cassandras, like Mr Winston Churchill, who were predicting doom and gloom. But by now Adolf had already marched into Austria and swallowed it up in one easy, almost bloodless, gulp. By 1939, when Fred Foster had reached the age of twenty-four, the cloud cast by what was now known as the Third Reich had darkened the whole of Europe. And though Thomas Cook, incredibly, was still turning out those cheery holiday brochures for Berlin and Vienna, for young men like Fred, the froth on the beer was about to go very flat.

On 5 May, he walked into the Territorial Army office in Newark and volunteered as a private in the 8th battalion of the Nottinghamshire and

Derbyshire regiment, colloquially known as the Sherwood Foresters. Over evenings and weekends during the long, beautiful summer of 1939, he underwent his basic training, culminating in an intensive two weeks at an army camp in north Wales. By now, few people had any illusions left; war with Germany seemed inevitable.

On 1 September, Germany invaded Poland, the last straw for Britain and France. On that same day the 8th Sherwood Foresters, like all territorial units, was embodied by Act of Parliament into the regular army, becoming part of the 148 Infantry Brigade. Fred's civilian life was now over. He said a final goodbye to the desk at Colton & Franks behind which he had sat for the last ten years and, like millions of others, put his personal dreams into cold storage. But the next day he found himself sitting behind a new desk. His professional experience had been noted and he was appointed clerk to the Brigade and raised in rank from private to lance-corporal.

On the morning of 3 September, a warm late summer Sunday, Harry Foster and his daughter Hilda sat waiting in the back parlour of 32 Bowbridge Road. The house seemed strange, just not right, knowing that Fred would not be coming home that night. Just after 11 o'clock, the voice of nice Mr Chamberlain came crackling out over their old wireless. It had started.

*

Two hundred-odd miles to the south, another family was gathered round the wireless. But this was a very different house to the one in Newark and a very different family.

The small town of New Milton sat snugly in the comfortable pastures of Hampshire, between Bournemouth to the west and Lymington to the east. The beauty of the New Forest was close by, as was the coast, with a long, sandy beach and glorious views out towards the Isle of Wight. New Milton sat a mile or so inland, holding itself back from the wild winds that could roar up the English Channel: the sort of place inhabited by people seeking unruffled lives. Behind the pretty High

Street, in the leafy avenues of detached houses, the respectable middle classes kept themselves to themselves. If they had any skeletons in their closets they would be firmly locked away and no light would ever be allowed to shine upon them.

In one of these avenues was the Villa Vita. Not quite as grand as its name suggests, it was nonetheless a fine, spacious residence. Today, it is surrounded by dull estates of 'executive' dwellings that have nibbled away at its once extensive gardens, but it remains a house that suggests its inhabitants have done well for themselves.

In the 1930s, the Villa Vita was the home of Captain John Coulthard, a former officer in the Royal Flying Corps, his wife Dorothy and their three children. The ethos inside its walls was as expansive and aspirational as Bowbridge Road was cramped and deadening. In fact, Captain and Mrs Coulthard were far from the conventional couple that their neighbours might have imagined them to be.

As with Fred Foster's lost mother, Dorothy seems to have been the dominant parent. Born in Bombay into a military family, she was highly intelligent, mercurial and feisty. Returning to Britain to be educated, she had gone on to become a private governess and then a qualified teacher. She had imbibed many 'modern' ideas, was sympathetic to the ideals of the socialist Fabian Society and had regularly rebelled against her authoritarian, right-wing father. This had come to a head in the early Thirties when, at a fateful Christmas lunch, she had praised the Labour Party, Hitler and German people. Her father had stormed out and they never spoke again. But Dorothy had good reason to cling to the hope of peace. In World War One, her brother had been killed and her husband had suffered badly from his time in the trenches as an infantry sergeant: his injuries had ended his active service career in the army and banished him to the safety of a desk job in the Royal Flying Corps (RFC). As her own children would find out, Dorothy believed in speaking her mind, whether or not you wanted to hear it.

Captain Coulthard himself had come from a humbler, though genteel, background, the son of a clergyman who had died young, leaving a widow with four young children. Extrovert and charismatic,

John had worked hard, reached London University and gained a degree in Mathematics. After the RFC, he had moved into teaching, rising gradually to become an Inspector of Schools.

This highly-intelligent couple both disliked the rigidities of the British class system. In the disaster at Gallipoli, John had seethed at the sight of easy promotion given to incompetent but well-connected officers. The Coulthards believed that education was the best weapon with which to tackle these injustices and improve opportunities for everyone. They also believed in gender equality and when they eventually produced a son and two daughters, it never occurred to them that the girls, Daphne and Pamela, should achieve anything less than the boy. But despite the elegance of the Villa Vita and the presence of a live-in maid to keep it spotless, the Coulthards were far from rich and, when the time came, pennies would definitely be pinched to help all three children through university.

This, then, was the middle-class family of high-achievers into which John Antony Ronald Coulthard, always called Antony, was born on 9 April 1918. After spells in Exeter and Stroud, the family eventually settled in New Milton and Antony was sent to the King Edward VI School in Southampton, one of the oldest schools in England. His parents expected him not just to work hard, but to shine brightly, and he did. Little quarter was given for slacking and none at all for failure. Like his sisters, he was to be the living, breathing proof of his parents' theory about the liberating power of a fine education.

Many years later, Antony's niece would opine that the love between John and Dorothy Coulthard and their children was not unconditional, but dependent on academic performance, on achieving the goals their parents had set them, whether or not they themselves wished to reach them. It is a hard judgment, but one that seems verified by the lifelong tensions within the family relationships. Expectations can be a heavy burden and no boy had greater expectations than Antony Coulthard.

But Antony did not disappoint them, academically at least. He took to study like a duck to water, enjoying it not just for its own sake but perhaps as a refuge from the sometimes strained atmosphere of the

Villa Vita. It soon turned out that he had a striking gift for languages, a fluke of fate that would turn out to shape the rest of his life.

He was a placid, easy-going boy of middling height, with a fair complexion, light brown hair and brown eyes. Chronically short-sighted, he was forced to wear horn-rimmed glasses, which he had a habit of taking off quickly to squint at the smallest letters of some text, holding it right up to his nose. Not much good at sport, he was almost the stereotypical classroom swot. Socially a bit gauche, the noisy back-slapping camaraderie of the rugby pitch was an alien place. Until his peers got to know him, he would seem quiet and reserved but, once they did, it was soon clear there was someone worth knowing behind the horn-rimmed glasses.

His passion for languages flowed logically into a fascination with the countries in which they were spoken. Germany especially captured his imagination and he became a fervent devotee of its history, litera-ture, art and music. The school magazine from 1936 describes the 'indefatigable Coulthard' giving an 'exhaustive lecture on western Germany, illustrated by innumerable lantern slides'. Later that year, he went off to study languages at The Queen's College, Oxford. This was partly funded by his having won not one but two scholarships, a fact no doubt welcomed by his parents and their bank manager. The quality of his intelligence was quickly recognised by his tutors; their admiration mixed in with an amused recognition of his absent-mindedness. Some friends from King Edward VI School who had also made it to the 'dreaming spires' sent occasional reports back to the school magazine. One stated: 'Antony approaches everything with tremendous concen-tration, whether it be German literature or a cow. In fact, so profoundly does he concentrate on some things that he totally forgets the existence of others. However, this is but the eccentricity of genius.'

That his academic worth was widely appreciated was lucky, because he was far less suited to the other aspects of Oxford life. Just as his father had baulked at the class-ridden elitism he had seen in the military, Antony was a middle-class boy surrounded by the upper-crust excesses of what we might now call 'the Brideshead thing'. The vacuous, spoiled 'toffs' of the Bullingdon Club, the white-tie college balls and the punting on the Cherwell were not exactly his scene, though it seems he made some small effort to fit in.

'Coulthard *has* been seen in the stern of a boat at times,' wrote a friend of Antony's half-hearted rowing, 'but his studious disposition usually keeps him otherwise engaged.'

He was well aware that Oxford was a privileged oasis in a country struggling through the desert of the worst economic downturn in anyone's memory. Imbued with his mother's Fabian principles and following in the footsteps of the ex-King Edward VIII (who decreed that 'something must be done'), he visited the grim mining communities of South Wales, where he stayed with a miner's family for part of his first Easter vacation. What they made of the earnest young student is anyone's guess. But it was an early sign of his desire to be able to talk to all sorts of people and to understand something of their lives, a virtue that would win him much affection in times to come.

But most of his time was still spent among the architecture of Wren and Hawksmoor; in particular inside the grand, neo-classical reading-rooms of the Taylorian Institute, that part of the Bodleian Library devoted to the study of modern European languages. Here he began to absorb everything it could feed him on Germany, a country whose epic history and culture continued to obsess him. The land of Beethoven, Schiller, Wagner and – above all – Goethe seemed to speak to something in Antony Coulthard's soul.

The various scholarships he had won entitled him to spend short periods studying there. The summer of 1937 found him in Magdeburg, the ancient university city on the River Elbe, founded by Charlemagne, where Martin Luther had gone to school. The following year he spent six weeks in an even more beautiful town in Hesse with the confusingly similar name of Marburg. Here was the picture-book essence of the old heroic Germany, where the Brothers Grimm had gathered many of their fairy tales. It was a place of cobbled, winding streets, houses with steep roofs and eccentric gables, a magnificent Gothic church and a castle on a hilltop high above a sleepy river. It was also an ancient seat of learning, the site of Germany's first Protestant University.

By this time, though, the old houses of Marburg were infested, like rats behind the skirting boards, with the plague of Nazism. The old market square had been renamed Adolf Hitler Platz. Many professors and tutors, and particularly Jews, had left the country since Hitler came to power in 1933. The Nazis, scared of people who thought for themselves, had introduced restrictions on the student population and their numbers in Marburg had dropped by over fifty percent. Antony was depressed to find that the nice lady with whom he lodged was a Nazi. In his small bedroom were framed photographs of both Hitler and Goering.

'Goering is posed with a feather in his tin hat,' he wrote to his mother, 'a double-barrelled shotgun slung over his shoulder, useful for purging the German forests of the foul non-Aryan. I do not shrink from shaking both fists at him every four hours.'

He tried hard to understand how the land of his hero Goethe had come to this sorry, philistine pass. But he soon found that the attitudes of the people were complicated. His cheery landlady for instance, whom he described as 'a treat', had once been the prosperous owner of a shoe shop, but now scratched out a scanty living for herself and her invalid daughter. Her business had been driven to bankruptcy by Jewish competition, yet she bore no grudge against Jews as a whole, in fact feeling sorry for the discrimination so many were now suffering at the hands of the Third Reich.

'She was largely uninterested in politics. Her allegiance to Nazism was inspired by the best in it and did not preclude all faculty of criticism.'

He even took a liking to the local Nazi party functionary who had come to dinner at his lodgings and made a fluent, compelling defence of National Socialism.

'I now realise it is possible for an educated German to approve of Nazism in general, whilst reserving the right to criticise in detail and shut their eyes to the grosser excesses.'

But his mother's Fabian principles and his own visit to the miner's family in South Wales had not dulled his sharp awareness of the differences that class structures often created.

'It is simply not true to say that the whole German people were so disgusted with the Weimar Republic that they welcomed the Nazis with open arms,' he wrote. 'But the general attitude of the common folk is one of relative indifference. If the peasant has a bad crop, he will blame Hitler for it; if a good one he will praise him.'

Marburg nevertheless worked its magic on him. His favourite place to study was on a balcony with a glorious view of the castle and the town huddled at its skirts, especially in the evening when the turreted silhouette stood out against the sunset. That summer, a festival of plays was presented on the castle hill, all of them Shakespeare. How easy it was to lull yourself into believing that, despite everything, Germany would never pose a threat to Britain.

The letter written to his mother from Marburg is remarkable: over eighty pages long, it not only covered his reflections on Germany, politics and economics, but was an astute analysis of his own character. Despite his academic achievements, he obviously felt that he fell short of being the ideal son. He defended himself against Dorothy's complaint that he was socially inept and lost in his own little world.

'If I am in the right mood… I am the life and soul of the party. I am astounded at the wealth of *bon mots* and humorous remarks I bring forth.'

He pleads however that he can only do this in 'sympathetic company. I mean people who combine an interest in serious matters with a sense of humour. The latter is even more essential than the former. If I find no response to my sense of humour then I shut up like an oyster.'

That Antony loved his mother is in no doubt. He always fretted about her constant insomnia. But it seems clear he does not always regard her as sympathetic.

'Conscious of my many grievous faults, always anticipating some new censure, I am, quite honestly, a little timid in your presence… I am much more depressed by my faults and failures than I am elated by my successes. Hence an inferiority complex.'

Chapter One

The paradox of this twenty-year-old boy is that, whilst claiming to suffer from low self-esteem, he was totally aware of his prodigious gifts and his worthiness to have a place at life's high table. The long letter from Marburg is permeated by this duality. Indeed, by this time, it might even be said that there were 'two Antonys'. One was the introverted boy from the Villa Vita, pushed hard all his life by well-meaning parents, but still feeling that, in their eyes at least, he would never be quite up to the mark whatever he achieved. And the other, the student from Oxford, liberated at last from their critical presence, flying free in the company of those of comparable intelligence and academic vigour.

In the quadrangles and the college halls, in the libraries and the tea rooms, he had gradually become more at ease with himself. The brilliant scholar who had started to bud in Southampton was blossoming into what could only be called an intellectual. He knew that, embraced it, wore it proudly on his sleeve. At last, his life had really started.

'Ever a steady rock in a surging sea,' wrote another friend at Christmas 1938, 'Coulthard continues to lead his customary industrious life, riding upon his bicycle to and from the Taylorian with an erectness which is positively military. Suffice it to mention his sacrifice when he donned once again the robes of Father Christmas at the German Club; again he burst into song wildly waving an egg-cup, thereby spilling its contents.'

Even this close to the outbreak of war, it seems that the golden students of Oxford University were happy to gather under the Christmas tree (a German creation), to drink schnapps and sing 'Stille Nacht, Heilige Nacht'. However clever they were, like millions of others, they too seem to have clung to Mr Chamberlain's flimsy piece of paper.

In that last Oxford summer of 1939, his old school in Southampton was informed that Antony, just turned twenty-one, was still working with a 'lion-like tenacity of purpose'. His reward was a BA with First Class Honours and special mention for his proficiency in colloquial German. This last facility would soon shape his destiny.

Only weeks after receiving his degree in the Sheldonian Theatre, with his proud parents and sisters looking on, the country of his birth was forced to declare war on the country he had come to love. It was as if Shakespeare were at war with Schiller, Elgar with Wagner, Byron with Goethe. But Antony Coulthard was not going to sit on any sort of spiritual fence. On 22 September 1939, he walked from The Queen's College, up the long avenue of St Giles, past his beloved Taylorian Library, to the recruitment office in Manor Road. Here he joined the Oxford & Buckinghamshire Light Infantry. As the son and grandson of military men, it is unlikely he had ever considered not joining up, but as heir to his parents' egalitarian views, he firmly refused a commission.

Like Fred Foster up in Newark, like those millions of young men perched on the cusp of life, it was far from the future he had expected. The boy with the glittering prizes within his grasp was now nothing more than a common soldier. He would not have had it any other way. But the years ahead would show just how uncommon the scholar in the horn-rimmed spectacles really was.

CHAPTER TWO

'**P**eggy, the world has gone mad. Let's go mad with it.'

On 24 February 1940, Fred Foster, in his best service dress, stood on the steps outside the church of St Mary's in Barnard Castle, County Durham. He had just married the most beautiful girl in the world. He still couldn't believe his luck, couldn't believe that Miss Peggy Urquhart, spinster, was now Mrs Frederick Foster.

Nobody else in the wedding photographs could quite believe it either. Behind the smiles, there was a shadow of concern. The newly-weds had only known each other a couple of months. Peggy's father, gassed in the trenches, had died just after the Great War and her grandfather had become, in these more patriarchal times, her *de facto* guardian. He had taken to Fred at once, but who wouldn't take to Fred Foster? Always charming and considerate to Peg's mother; always happy to go for a pint with her grandad and talk about the football.

All the same, it had happened a bit fast. So fast, in fact, that the photographs clearly show a slight bulge in Fred's breast pocket, later revealed to be a packet of letters from a girl in Newark to whom he had been unofficially engaged and who had now been jilted in favour of the red-haired belle of Barnard Castle. It was a sartorial oversight he would not be allowed to forget in the fifty years of their marriage.

As in all the best romances they had met on a train. Peggy was heading home from her work as a student paediatric nurse near

London; she was a bright girl, had been to grammar school. Fred was returning from Newark to Barnard Castle where, since October 1939, he'd been billeted while his brigade was trained for future deployment. His qualities had continued to be appreciated. He had risen to become the brigade chief clerk and had already won his sergeant's stripes.

It was still the so-called 'Phoney War', the autumn and winter months following Mr Chamberlain's sad declaration, when no further land offensives took place in western Europe. The opposing sides were like two angry dogs, pawing the ground with teeth bared, but neither yet making that first vicious leap. In Britain, daily life seemed to go on much as before but it was a superficial normality. Everyone knew that the future could not be counted on. The philosophy that would come to dominate so many people's thinking for the next five years was already taking root. Live for the moment. Grab your happiness while you can. For young people, especially young men who knew they would soon be sent to fight and perhaps to die, the previous route map of their lives had now become useless. Who knew any longer where their road was to take them and how long or short that road might be?

The generation before them had known these emotions only too well. They'd lived through the last time the world had torn itself apart. Now that the same thing was, incredibly, happening again, they could hardly be censorious of those same feelings in their sons and daughters. So, as they stood on the church steps, whatever doubts or worries the parents may have had were kept to themselves. Besides, it was plain to see that Peggy Urquhart and Fred Foster were head over heels. For the two young strangers on the train, it seems to have been a *coup de foudre*, a bolt of lightning.

Fred was nearly twenty-five now. He might not have been Clark Gable, but he wasn't that bad a catch. The bricklayer's son had risen to become the senior articled clerk in the solicitor's office, a solid respectable job. There had been quite a few girls more than willing to 'walk out' with Fred Foster. So when he met the beautiful redhead from Barnard Castle, he was more than able to make a comparative judgment. His judgement being that here, on a dull, wintry journey, as the train steamed its way to the north, was the girl he would love for the rest of his life. And he wasn't going to let her get away.

'We've no money, no home, nothing but each other. I'm like a lost soul without you' he wrote when she'd gone back south to her work as a nurse. 'Some other Fred would say, "You're heading for disaster"; this one says, "You love that girl. You're marrying her."'

There was no time to waste. A special licence was obtained. The invitations were sent out. Peggy Urquhart walked down the aisle of St Mary's on her grandfather's arm and walked back up it as the wife of a soldier. If this was madness, Fred thought, it was the sanest thing he had ever done.

But all the bright smiles and the flashes of the camera couldn't quite dispel the reality of their situation. As the bride and groom were toasted at a modest reception in her mother's small house, Fred knew that, finally, his own 'Phoney War' was over. The 148th Infantry Brigade of former territorials, consisting of the 8th Sherwood Foresters and the 5th Leicesters, was about to be posted abroad. His time with Peggy, those painfully short precious months, was running out. The sand was trickling through the hourglass at an ever faster rate.

Fred was proud to be in the Sherwood Foresters, an ancient regiment with an illustrious history. Its men had fought against Napoleon in the Peninsular War and in the Crimea at Inkerman and Sebastopol. In the Great War, it had won seven Victoria Crosses and the great Allied commander Marshal Foch had praised it, saying, 'You have the courage of lions, the impossible has been asked of you and you have done it.'

Though Fred was the brigade's chief clerk, there was no way he could remain protected from danger behind a desk. The months of training at Barnard Castle were to teach the clerks, the schoolteachers, the factory workers, the farm labourers, the miners and the bus drivers how to be fighting men. In this, too, as well as in affairs of the heart, there was hardly enough time. Britain was racing to get its forces up to speed for whatever might be coming its way and, if Hitler's recent record was anything to go by, that might even include invasion.

In April 1940, however, the Germans turned their guns on Norway instead and, for the British Tommy, the beautiful land of mountains and fjords was destined to be the first theatre of World War Two. As Hitler gradually overshadowed Europe, Norway had struggled hard to maintain a position of neutrality, but this had become increasingly untenable. Apart from merely expanding the Germanic empire, the Nazis wanted occupation of Norway's ice-free ports for easy access to Sweden's iron ore and to underpin its control of the North Atlantic. On 9 April, the Germans invaded. King Olav begged the British for help.

Only five weeks after Peggy became a bride, she found herself effectively single again. Painful farewells were said on the platform at Barnard Castle, that same station to which they'd been travelling on the day they'd met, just five months before. They had always known this moment would come, but not how awful it would be when it did. All around them, dozens of other wives, sweethearts and parents were playing out the same tearful scene. But there were brave smiles and words of reassurance. The whole thing would be over in a few months. It looked like old Winston might soon be in charge; he'd get this mess sorted out. Then the troop train pulled slowly away, a hundred arms waving wildly from its windows, leaving behind the sad sisterhood of women without men.

If Peggy Foster had known just what her husband was now heading towards, her fears for him would have been even greater. In almost every way, Norway could hardly have presented a more difficult challenge. The British forces, so hurriedly pulled together, were nearly all territorial units; the regular army was massed in France waiting for Hitler's expected invasion. By now, the former territorials were passably trained, but nobody would have claimed they were crack troops. Worse, such was the necessary haste that when Fred's brigade set sail from Rosyth on 17 April, it was at only fifty percent of its required strength. Then, halfway across the North Sea, the merchant ship carrying their anti-tank artillery, communications equipment, Arctic clothing, Bren carriers and vital food supplies was torpedoed and took the whole lot to the bottom. They arrived near Lillehammer on 18 April, half crippled before they'd even taken their first steps on Norwegian soil.

These were the men who were about to see the first serious action of World War Two. No doubt they were excited, gung-ho even, eager to do their duty for King and country. No doubt Fred had been cracking jokes in his usual way as they crossed the sea. Alongside him were plenty of lads he'd known back home, boys he'd grown up with. Among these was a young lieutenant named Jack Esam, a year older than Fred who, by coincidence, had worked as a solicitor in a law practice just along the street from Fred's own firm. Over the years the two had got to know each other well. But in among the jokes and the joshing, there must have been fear, too. Not that any of them would have shown it. Nobody wanted it getting back to Newark that they'd been 'frit'.

If they had been, they'd have had good reason. The job of the 148th Infantry Brigade was to support the overwhelmed Norwegian Army in trying to stop the Nazi advance north from Oslo. It was a doomed enterprise. The very next day, they made contact with the German armoured forces and were compelled to stage a fighting withdrawal to allow the tattered, weary remnants of the Norwegian forces to pass through their positions and try to regroup.

So began four long, hellish days of fighting in Arctic conditions, hopelessly under-armed and with very little food. In next to no time, young Fred Foster had gone from the warmth of Peggy's arms to a frozen hell of destruction and death. The contrast must have seemed like some unbelievable nightmare. They'd had enough training to know how they must behave and respond, but no training could possibly have prepared them for their first experience of violent armed combat.

The brigade made a stand near the village of Tretten, to prevent a vital bridge falling into German hands and cutting off the retreating Norwegian forces. The Sherwood Foresters, with the help of some Norwegian civilians, prepared defensive positions among the rocky outcrops on the heights above the bridge. The digging of trenches was impossible because they had no tools with which to penetrate the frozen ground. Meanwhile, the Leicesters continued to engage the advancing Germans in order to buy time for the defences to be constructed.

What became known as the Battle of Tretten Gorge began early on 23 April, the anniversary of Agincourt. But this was never going to be another English triumph. The odds were just too large. The troops in forward positions were soon overrun as tanks and supporting infantry ploughed through them in their push north towards the village and the precious bridge. Armed only with their basic rifles, their limited ammunition already running out, the Foresters were subjected to continuous mortar and machine-gun fire, from both armoured and ski troops, as they tried to give cover for the defeated remnants of the forward positions to fall back. Eventually, things descended into hand-to-hand fighting, but the battle was lost.

By around 9pm, both the village and the bridge had finally been taken by the Germans. The Brigadier now asked for volunteers to form a token rearguard to stay behind, hold the road and cover the retreat of the British forces. It was a pretty short straw but among those with the courage to take it were the two lads from the solicitors' office in Newark, Sergeant Fred Foster and Lieutenant Jack Esam. How weird to be together now on this rocky hillside so far from home: a place where precious little justice could be expected. A fact the Nazis were about to prove in the most brutal way possible.

Suddenly, like some lumbering monster, a German tank came round a corner. The British dashed for cover in the trees, but then a voice came from the tank, speaking in English, saying, 'Come out Englishmen, it is all right.' Knowing they were cornered with no chance of escape, Lieutenant Esam went slowly forward to surrender. They shot him dead. Another soldier who ran to his aid was similarly cut down, after which the tank sprayed the treeline with fire. Very few escaped but Fred Foster was one.

Almost till the end, small pockets of Sherwood Foresters went on fighting on the heights above the village but they were soon silenced in one way or another. More German tanks gave chase, against which the British weaponry was as useless as a nail-file. The tanks opened fire at almost point-blank range and hardly a man was left standing. To make sure the job was done, the Germans jumped down from the tanks and shot each of the wounded in the head. No prisoners were taken. It was cold-bloodied execution. The first German war crime of World War Two.

Before the guns at last fell silent, 148th Infantry Brigade had ceased to exist as a fighting unit. Most of its men were killed, wounded or captured. Out of a force of about fourteen hundred, only around two hundred men and a few officers managed to escape to the north and return to Britain. For the sake of morale, the extent of the catastrophe was kept from the British public. Britain's first military strike against the Nazis could hardly have gone any worse.

But the young sergeant from Newark, still so wet behind the ears, had acted bravely. He had kept on doing his job even though he'd just seen a man he knew well cut down like a dog, his blood splattered over the frozen hillside. Eventually Fred was wounded in the leg and captured. It had been his first experience of action and, though he couldn't yet know it, would also be his last.

It is not clear how Fred Foster and those of his comrades who survived Tretten Gorge were taken into captivity in Nazi-occupied Poland. It may have been on the notorious cattle-truck trains or mostly by sea to a German port on the Baltic coast. But at least he was alive. Unlike Jack Esam, he might one day go back to Newark, not in a wooden box but proudly and on his own two feet. But that day was to be a very long way off.

'I think your prayers for me must have been answered,' he would later write to his bride, 'as how I escaped with my life, I do not know. Our love is something that governments, shells and bullets cannot take away from me. Something which, if I *had* gone with some of the boys, I should have taken into eternity with me.'

For the moment, however, the reality of capture, in all its desolation, had to be faced. Only seventeen days after leaving Peggy, Fred Foster was a German prisoner of war. He was not to see her again for five years.

*

It is a nice photograph. In black and white of course. A young man and woman standing on a small bridge beside a lake in what looks to be a park or perhaps the grounds of some country house. They stand slightly apart and it is hard to guess what their relationship might be. The boy is Antony Coulthard; the girl is unknown, lost in time. Perhaps she is just a girl from college or a friend of the family; some distant cousin perhaps. Someone of no particular importance to him.

But how pleasing it would be if that were not the case. How good to know, in the light of what was to happen, that Antony had carried some special face with him as he went towards the war; that the human emotions he read about on the pages of books had also touched him in person. It would be sad to think that, sitting in his Oxford ivory tower, enthralled by the boundless horizons of the mind, he had neglected those of the heart, perhaps thinking that there was plenty of time for all that in the future.

In short, just as Fred Foster had his Peggy, did Antony Coulthard have a sweetheart, too? Was there somebody who had diverted him from the aspirational treadmill, from the compulsion to achieve what his parents had imposed on him since childhood? It is sentimental to hope that he experienced shy kisses in the evening shadows of the quad or on the banks of the Cherwell, but one hopes for it just the same. Unlike in the case of Fred, there is no treasure trove of love letters, so we shall never know. What is certain is that somehow, in the remaining years of his life, in the grim circumstances in which he was to find himself, Antony would prove that his heart was easily the equal of his head.

But when World War Two began, it was the latter that was wanted. The recruiting officers in the city of dreaming spires must have been frustrated by the number of clever young men like Antony Coulthard who, as a matter of principle, refused a commission and reduced themselves to the ranks. What a waste, they thought. If it was to defeat Hitler, Britain needed their brainpower. But the recruiting officers would not allow themselves to be totally obstructed and Antony was quickly transferred from the Oxford and Bucks Light Infantry into the Field Security Police, known as the Green Caps, where his expertise in languages was seen as a hugely valuable asset. By mid-1940, the old FSP would be swallowed up into the newly formed Intelligence Corps and it was as a founder member of this that Antony would in future be listed.

The very same week that Fred and Peggy Foster were saying their goodbyes on the platform at Barnard Castle, Antony Coulthard was doing the same at the Villa Vita in Hampshire. How hard it must have been for his parents in particular. Captain Coulthard had survived the Great War, but not without scars of both types. Dorothy had lost her younger brother to the trenches. And now their brilliant boy, the cynosure of their ambition, was being so cruelly ripped away from the future they had wanted for him. Neither could believe they had lived to see all this happening again.

The day after he left home, he sent a last letter to his mother from his billet, revealing again that the relationship between them was complex but still loving.

'I shall always be thinking of you and pondering your many words of wisdom and sound advice, which I only *appear* to ignore,' he wrote. 'The months will soon roll by until I am home again on leave.'

It was not to be.

After only three weeks' training, Antony was made an acting Lance Corporal and embarked for France to join the intelligence services at Brest on the northwest coast of Brittany. In the middle of May, he was transferred to 32 Field Security Section in Rennes, which was attached to the 45th Division of the British Expeditionary Force, the name given to the first wave of British troops in western Europe during the months between the British declaration of war on Germany and the fall of France and subsequent evacuation at Dunkirk.

Just two days after arriving in Rennes, he was sent on a long motorcycle reconnaissance mission right across northern France to Amiens in the east. His objective was to establish the whereabouts of a Divisional Headquarters that had become uncertain. At first, he seems to have had quite a nice trip, almost a bit of a holiday. In Rouen, he spent a pleasant spring Sunday seeing the sights, exploring the vast Gothic cathedral and touring around on his motorbike. It was almost as if all was well with the world.

The next morning he set out with another of his corps to try and track down the elusive unit to which they were now to be attached. The further east they travelled, the more the reality of war forced itself into their consciousness. The holiday was over. The Nazis were coming. As they headed towards Amiens, the roads became ever more crowded with endless columns of refugees, loaded down with all their possessions, fleeing from the encroaching German forces now pushing westwards at terrifying speed. These were roads that the German bombers had recently strafed, leaving huge craters, smouldering carts and horses with horrible wounds. Worse of all were the corpses of all ages and both sexes, barely recognisable now as human beings. One presumes it was the first time this twenty-one year old had seen violent death.

Much later, he would write a long explanation home of what exactly happened next.

'At Montdidier, which was practically deserted, my leaking petrol tank ran dry. I managed to beg some from a French lorry. They told us that Amiens had been heavily bombed for two days in succession. Arriving at Roye, we were warned by a French Artillery General against going further along the road than the last French outposts. A despatch rider now told us that our unit had been stationed at Doullens, and it was necessary to pass by Amiens to reach it. The road that fateful evening of 20 May was straight and deserted. The villages, too, had been practically deserted. The only incident, before we came into view of the red glow and pall of smoke that overhung Amiens, was that my companion ran over a calf.'

It is hard not to wish they had listened to the French General, turned their bikes around and roared back westwards towards some sort of safety. But they were British soldiers and they had orders to join their unit. Turning tail was not in their psychology, though the ultimate sight of Amiens must have been a shock.

Chapter Two

'The town itself was a scene of desolation: fallen masonry, broken-down tram wires, debris of all kinds scattered over the streets and an eerie silence, broken only by the distant crackling of the flames that reddened the fading sky. Curiosity led me on. What could there be to fear anyway, in a deserted city? We should surely meet Allied troops soon. The enemy was at least twenty miles away.'

On that score, he could not have been more wrong.

'Rounding a bend in the centre of the town, I spotted some motorcyclists in long military mackintoshes and a helmet that was certainly not British and not recognisably French. It was a moment before the awful truth dawned on me – it seemed so impossible! Once I realised it, however, I resigned myself to the inevitable. What use was it for me, unarmed and inexperienced on a motorbike, to cut and run? Probably most of the roads were blocked. So I just carried on till summoned to stop. I could hear my companion's machine coming round the bend about five hundred yards behind me. I have never seen him since, so whether he got killed or escaped I cannot say. My captors were amazed to find my holster empty (our pistols had been collected before I left Brest and never re-issued). They escorted me away on my bike, but as it conked out and refused to start again I had to push it till it was taken from me and given to one of the younger German soldiers.'

It was hardly a heroic surrender. An empty holster and a broken-down bike with a leaking petrol tank. It was a sad metaphor for the doomed attempt of the Allied forces to stop the Third Reich taking control of western Europe. Within a six-week period from 10 May 1940, Hitler would occupy the Netherlands, Luxembourg, Belgium and France. Compared to the sleek, modern Nazi war machine, the British Expeditionary Force was woefully ill equipped and under-trained. In the 1930s, Britain hadn't listened to Winston Churchill shouting from the wilderness. When they finally did, it was just a bit too late. The BEF was surrounded and chased till they were left stranded on the beaches of Dunkirk, desperately awaiting evacuation. Luckily, for most of them, rescue would come. Had he turned that old motorbike around and at least taken a crack at escaping from Amiens, Antony Coulthard might conceivably have been one of them.

The question arises why he didn't. Did he really believe, as he states, that it was a useless gesture and that he might have ended up with a bullet in his back? Or did he find something noble, irresistible even, in the theatrical gesture of riding onwards straight into their arms? It seems certain that there was an impulsive streak in his make-up which, despite his intelligence, would sometimes lead him into reckless behaviour, both then and in the future.

Anyway, the die was cast. He was now a German prisoner of war. One wonders what the feeling was like when, in simply driving round a street corner, the route of your life is changed in a moment from that of a free man with a free will to being in total subjugation to the will of strangers. And not just any strangers, but those who wish you harm. In World War Two, around 200,000 Allied soldiers would know that moment.

The first long night of Antony Coulthard's captivity was passed in a large building, probably some school, on the outskirts of the still smouldering Amiens. He was certainly far from alone. A couple of hundred other British soldiers were being held there, too: both officers and other ranks, mostly militiamen and territorials who, armed with just rifles and a few Bren guns, had resisted the dreadful onslaught of German artillery, tanks and aircraft that afternoon. Their intelligence sources had led them to expect no more than a few German parachutists and their casualties had been heavy. There were also the remnants of the Royal Sussex Battalion who had been blown to pieces as their train drew into Amiens station two days before.

'Intermittent gunfire could be heard in the distance, but otherwise the night was calm,' he wrote.

It is hard to believe he could have felt calm inside. He must have had some vague idea of what awaited him, though perhaps imagination was worse. In any event, it would be his last quiet night for some time. The next morning, wide awake, his nightmare was to begin. His march into captivity would last nine long days.

Chapter Two

'Those nine days were, I think, the worst of my life,' he wrote afterwards. 'I had a greatcoat and a full pack on my back under the sweltering sun. It made my heart bleed to have to leave my blankets, ground sheet and motorcycling kit, all of which would have been invaluable on the road. Still, I salvaged all my personal kit.'

Some of the time, they progressed on foot, covering seventeen miles on that first day. At other times, they were moved forward in rickety old lorries. Rarely, however, did they have any shelter. By day, they baked in the sunshine; their skin burnt raw by the sun, their throats parched, their feet throbbing with blisters. By night, they froze in open fields as, mile by weary mile, they edged across Belgium towards the border with the Third Reich itself. By now, they were becoming familiar with a physical sensation most had never experienced before in their young lives. It was a feeling they soon became used to and one that would rarely leave them for the next five years: that gnawing and yearning in the guts called hunger.

The endless columns were a pitiable sight and pity was taken. French and Belgian civilians living along the route did their best to help in small ways. But since the Germans had overrun their homelands, their lives, too, were now frightening and uncertain. To be caught helping the POWs could only make that worse. But, by throwing some bread to the prisoners, or just by leaving a bucket of drinking water in plain sight as they passed through, a sense of human fellowship prevailed.

If the German guards saw the bucket, too, there was a good chance it would be kicked over. There was considerable brutality. Anyone who resisted their ill treatment would be beaten, whipped, or even shot dead on the spot. The younger guards were the worst. Already drunk on the mythology of Hitler and the Thousand-Year Reich, their all-conquering swagger across western Europe had intoxicated them even further.

But by far the worst was yet to come.

'Between St Vith, where we boarded the train at 2pm on 27 May, and Torun, which we reached on the evening of the 29th, forty of us were entombed in a cattle truck, alternately rattling and crawling through Moselland, Rhineland, Hessen, Thuringia and Saxony to a destination unknown. We seemed to spend more time in sidings than on the move. From time to time, we were let out to relieve nature; occasionally we received a ladleful of greasy soup.'

In the twenty-first century, the cattle-truck trains are most familiar to us from horrific documentaries about the transportation of Europe's Jews to the Nazi death camps, but they were also used to carry prisoners of war. No more than forty men were supposed to travel inside each truck (so Antony was quite lucky), but the Germans frequently crammed in fifty, sixty or more. They were often locked in for the best part of a day or even longer. The conditions grew hellish. There were no windows, only a few narrow slits a couple of inches high and about a foot wide. So there was air, but not nearly enough and it soon became stale and foetid. Nor were there any toilet facilities, not even a bucket. People resorted to urinating or defecating in their helmets or their boots and throwing it out through the slit; those with dysentery couldn't always manage even that and the floor was sometimes awash with diarrhoea.

The humiliation must have been intense. Their dehumanisation from free men to captives had begun. Sleep, the balm they all needed so badly, was hard to come by. The overcrowding meant that lying down was impossible, even sitting wasn't easy. If you were fortunate, you might snatch a nap squashed into some tight corner, propped shoulder to shoulder with somebody else, but the noise and shaking of the train, the stench of faeces and the hunger echoing in your belly might well put paid to that. For the fastidious middle-class boy from the Villa Vita and The Queen's College, Oxford, it must have been grim.

The poignancy of his situation would hardly have escaped him. Antony was back in Germany, but the country he had eagerly embraced not so long ago now had him in a totally involuntary grip. The land of Goethe and Beethoven had taken on a different face, though on the surface of course, it looked much the same. When the prison train reached Marburg, where he had spent a student summer just three years before, he caught glimpses through the slit of the hilltop castle he had known so well. It was a dreadful way to return. Here, miraculously, the prisoners were allowed out of the cattle-truck to stretch their legs, find a tree to urinate behind and be given watery coffee served by Red Cross nurses. One wonders if he recognised any local faces. A girl he'd once spoken to in a *bierkeller*? A German guard who'd lived in the street where Antony had once lodged?

It would seem that at this point in the trek east, he had a stroke of luck, somehow infiltrating a column of the sick who were being sent on ahead in lorries. By this means, he reached his destination more quickly and safely than so many of those who'd started the march with him across the dusty roads of Belgium. Nevertheless, the experience had marked him. He never forgot those who had never finished the journey, their dead bodies hauled out of the cattle-truck and left for someone, anyone, to bury.

'We shall all long remember the hunger, the thirst, the heat and fatigue, the cold nights, the queues for a mouthful of soup, the stampede for water.'

But his destination was not what he expected. This prison transport, among the earliest of World War Two, had gone right across Germany and over its eastern border into Nazi-occupied Poland. It did not stop till it reached the old medieval city of Torun, on the River Vistula. Here, in great haste, a POW camp had been established in a ring of old forts on the outskirts of the town.

When Antony Coulthard was marched into his new billet, it must have looked bleak beyond imagining. Barbed wire, armed sentries, swastikas draped everywhere. The only cheer for the new arrivals was the welcome of those British Tommies who'd got here before them, many from the catastrophic Norwegian campaign. These men, too, had had a rough journey to this miserable place and knew only too well how exhausted, hungry and desolate their new companions must be. As best they could, they reached out to give some help and comfort, especially to those who seemed most frail. A cheery handshake, a pat on the back, a corny joke.

'Welcome to the Hotel Torun. The porter will take your luggage.'

One of these 'old hands' went up to Lance Corporal Coulthard.

'Hello there' he said. 'My name's Fred Foster. You stick with me chum. I'll get you fixed up.'

CHAPTER THREE

The first weeks and months of their captivity were the worst.

Letters from home, that most treasured lifeline to a world that had been lost, had not yet begun to come through with any regularity. In Bowbridge Road, at the Villa Vita and in homes all over Britain, families were still waiting desperately for news, not knowing whether their husband, son, father or brother was alive, dead or in enemy hands. In that context, the armada of little boats that had brought back the tattered rump of the British Expeditionary Force from Dunkirk had also returned with gossip, rumour, mistaken belief and downright error.

'Please break the news gently to Peggy that I fear Fred is posted missing,' his sister Hilda wrote from Newark to Peggy's grandfather in Barnard Castle. Because Newark was the headquarters of the Sherwood Foresters, this was where any information arrived first.

'I know a gentleman whose son has got home and he says Fred is missing. I find comfort in Ribbentrop's statement to the press last week that they had captured the staff of 148th Brigade and tell Peggy I have the feeling that it's true. We are all very anxious. Give my love to Peggy. I will write to her soon but I thought *you* would break it gently.'

For an agonising period, Peggy could not be certain whether or not she was a war widow. The darkest moment was when those survivors of the Norwegian calamity made it back to Newark, passing through Barnard Castle. Naturally, she tried to reach these men and ask if they knew anything about Sergeant Foster. She did not receive the answer she hoped for. One man hesitantly told her he thought he had seen Fred lying dead outside a church where the regimental aid post had been established, but that he couldn't be absolutely certain. No doubt the soldier felt it was right to tell her, but the impact can be imagined. She could hardly sleep, hardly eat. How difficult it must have been to walk past St Mary's Church where, little more than two months before, she and Fred had stood together, near bursting with joy.

It would be several tortured weeks before Peggy got definite confirmation that her new husband was not lying dead outside a Norwegian church or on some cold slab of hillside, but was now a 'guest of Adolf'. The happy news made it into the local paper, which remarked that 'it will be a source of satisfaction to his many friends'. No doubt that was true and a good few glasses were raised to his health in the blacked-out public houses of Newark. Presumably, the paper had also reported the death of Lieutenant Jack Esam. We do not know if the two families ever met, either by design or by simply bumping into each other in the street. What on earth would they have said? In one home blessed relief, in the other, devastation. Such was the random cruelty of war.

In the days after the battle, Fred's overwhelming concern had been to let Peggy know he was all right but his first postcard took a long time reaching Barnard Castle, by which time she had received official notification of his capture. He wrote again on 18 May from the prison camp. Allowed only one page on which to write, he squeezed in as many words as he could.

'Write me every day dear, great long letters. I can send two a month with occasional postcards. Every time I write, please let Dad know darling.'

But there was also an urgent matter to be addressed.

'Pegs, will you please send me straight away a parcel containing: 2 handkerchiefs, I razor, 12 blades, lather brush, shaving soap, toilet soap, nail brush, toothbrush, toothpaste, 4lbs Cadbury's Plain Milk Chocolate, 1 tin of treacle, 2lb slab of fruitcake, white loaf, ½lb margarine, cigarettes, matches and any other nourishing food you can think of to make up a parcel. Please ask Dad to make me up a parcel as well and tell him to get our relatives to send me parcels. I need as many as possible. It is imperative I get parcels through. I'm afraid my darling, this has not left much room in which to tell you of my great love for you.'

There was good reason for the urgency in his voice. The lifeline of Red Cross parcels, which in time would make the POW's existence almost bearable and indeed save many from death, had not yet got underway. Tens of thousands like Fred Foster and Antony Coulthard, having somehow survived their ghastly journeys across Europe, now faced conditions they had never imagined having to endure in the middle of the twentieth century. It was as if the basic structures of a civilised life had been whipped from under their feet. But it was to be nearly three long, almost unendurable months before any reply from Peggy got through to Fred in his prison.

It was a painful paradox that the place in which Fred and Antony now found themselves was one of the most beautiful in northern Europe.

Torun, on the River Vistula about a hundred miles northwest of Warsaw, was a small city of Gothic grandeur. Its old quarter, on the northern bank of the river, boasted a magnificent cathedral where the astronomer Copernicus had been christened, a noble town hall, a grand market square, and wide streets of fine old houses. It had been a town in which anyone would have wanted to live and, far in the future, it would be that again. But for now, like the rest of Poland, it had fallen under the Nazi jackboot. Those of its people who had fought back had been hunted down and executed; the rest were cowed, frightened and hopeless. Still, though, there was some pale illusion of normality; some vestige of daily life went on.

But it was a tale of two cities. On the opposite bank of the wide, placid Vistula, things were to be very different. In the mid-19th century, Bismarck had ordered the building of six defensive forts on the

flatlands south of the river to defend Prussia against the threat from
Russia. These grim and crumbling buildings were now to form one
of the major POW camps of World War Two. Its formal name would
be Stalag XXA.

Under the German POW system, prisoners were segregated by
rank. Captured officers were kept in entirely separate camps called
Oflags, where they had little to do apart from strolling around, smoking
pipes and cursing The Hun. Men with the rank of sergeant or below
were confined in Stalags and required to work. To our modern sensi-
bilities, such 'class' inequality is jaw-dropping but, in its time, it seems
to have been somehow acceptable to the military psyche.

Stalag XXA, therefore, was designed to be a camp for the common
man. Under the terms of The 1929 Geneva Convention on the treatment of prisoners of war, the ordinary serviceman was required to do
any work he was physically able to perform, as long as it was not
dangerous and did not support the German war effort and thus under-
mine their own side. In practice, however, the definition of what did or
did not fall under this definition was a 'grey area'. It was also difficult
to police and the Germans regularly cocked a snook at the Geneva
Convention. So POWs were used in mining, quarrying and farming,
in sawmills and breweries, in the railway yards and in factories, all of
which at least indirectly supported the Nazi war machine. If the prisoners hadn't done those jobs, German men would have been required
and thus could not have been called up.

In Stalag XXA, the old Prussian forts were to be the main prisons
but, as the war went on and many more captives had to be accommo-
dated, satellite camps, of the wooden hut variety, had to be quickly
constructed nearby. Each of the forts, though very similar in design,
was given its own distinct usage. Fort 17, nearest to the town's railway
station, was used as a 'sorting office', where new arrivals were registered
as POWs, directed towards welcome showers, then allocated to a
specific fort or to one of the satellite camps. Fort 14 was, ultimately, the
hospital with a hundred beds, to be staffed by volunteer medics from
among the prison population. Fort 15 housed a mixed population of

Americans, Australians, New Zealanders, French and Italians, but would also eventually be used as a punishment camp for British RAF men from officers' camps in the surrounding area.

Not far from this main prison city, but separate from it, was Stalag XXC where mainly Soviet prisoners were kept. This was the bleakest place of all, where hard labour, starvation and epidemics combined to create the highest death rate of all. In World War Two, over three million Russian soldiers died in German prison camps. The excuse was later used that Russia had not signed up to the Geneva Convention and therefore their soldiers could be treated without any semblance of humanity. So much of Nazi ideology was based on racism and, in their view, the ordinary Russian soldier, the peasant from the Steppes, was the lowest form of life (it was not a view that would carry much weight five years later in the war crimes trials at Nuremberg).

By contrast, they had a higher regard for the British who, enemy or not, were an Aryan race and therefore worthy of a grudging racial respect. Fort 13, the largest of the old buildings, where Antony Coulthard and Fred Foster met for the first time in late May 1940, was designated as the British fort. At this point, Stalag XXA was in its infancy. The Germans had perhaps surprised themselves by the relative ease with which they had devoured Europe. Norway, The Netherlands, Belgium and finally France had fallen like dominoes and the Third Reich wasn't exactly ready for the massive influx of prisoners this would bring in its wake. In the new prison city of Torun, the structures necessary for an acceptable standard of living were barely in place. Facilities for cooking, laundry and hygiene were rudimentary to say the least. It was a bit like going on a holiday abroad and finding that the hotel was a dump and only half-built. And the 'Hotel Torun' was grossly overcrowded, at one point containing nearly twenty thousand men.

Most recently used by the Poles as barracks, the old forts were far from congenial spaces. In order to be camouflaged from any advancing army, the Prussians had scooped out the earth so that the brick and stone buildings were partially subterranean; their only windows were at the front, the rear was tunnelled into the ground. Only the roofs were at ground level, but these, too, were covered in earth; grass, shrubs and even trees were growing on top to disguise the complex from the air.

Sentry boxes guarded the formidable main gates, outside of which, bizarrely, was an area of manicured garden, with plants and flowers laid out in geometric patterns around embedded Swastikas. Within the gates, the original moat had long since been drained; thirty feet wide and fifty feet deep, it was now to be used as a parade ground for the daily roll call.

The main entrance to Fort 13 was via a drawbridge that spanned the moat. Beyond this, a long underground tunnel led into the gloomy depths of the building. Off it were dank, dark chambers, with vaulted ceilings, bare brick walls several feet thick and two small windows overlooking the dry moat. Each room was no more than about thirty feet by fifteen but would often house fifty or sixty men. They were depressing, sunless places; ice-cold in winter and, even in high summer, never entirely dry. A pair of boots left uncovered at lights out might be covered in mildew by morning. There were no proper 'beds'; they slept on three-tiered, shelf-like spaces with only a *palliasse*, a thin mattress inadequately stuffed with straw or sawdust, and two thin blankets. In the morning, the air had become so stale with the carbon dioxide of so many people that most woke up with a daily headache. Each room had a stove, but only one bucket of coal a day was provided and winter temperatures could dive as low as 30F below zero. For the prisoners, most of whom were to be undernourished for the next five years, it was about as unhealthy a place as could be imagined.

On arrival at Stalag XXA, the men were not interrogated about anything of a military nature, merely registered as POWs, as the Geneva Convention required. The only question they would have to answer was about their trade or profession in civilian life, so that they could be assigned to any suitable work party. As already noted, Stalag XXA was a 'work camp', an *Arbeitskommando*. Its inmates, however cold, tired, hungry or thirsty, were required to labour at whatever jobs were thrust upon them. To prop up the Third Reich, the prisoners might be sent out as farm workers or miners. Or to work on the railway tracks, unloading the barges on the river or breaking stones in the local quarries. Conditions in the work parties were usually harder than in the main camp. So men like Antony Coulthard and Fred Foster, whose qualifications were cerebral rather than physical, were sometimes luckier than most. Not always, though: if fifty men were required on a job, then fifty men would be supplied even if the heaviest thing they'd ever lifted had been the complete works of Shakespeare.

It was tough to exist on a calorie intake that would hardly satisfy a field mouse. In the early months especially, food was scarce and the water supply less than adequate. Every morning, the working day had to be powered on no more than a cup of coffee substitute. At midday, they got a bowl of watery vegetable soup with a loaf of sour-tasting bread to be divided between five or six men. In the evening, it was much the same again. Once or twice a week, the piss-poor soup might be fortified with a small portion of horsemeat or the bread garnished with margarine or honey. Somehow, the prisoners learnt to cope with these starvation rations. But the hunger was always there. Their bodies responded by burning up whatever reserves they still possessed and the weight fell off them. Big, strapping British lads saw themselves shrivel like a balloon pricked with a pin.

Illnesses were common and sometimes rampant. The health of many men had been seriously weakened by the horrors of their long journey into captivity. Some never entirely recovered. The most frequent complaints included dysentery, diphtheria and rheumatic conditions caused or exacerbated by the damp living quarters. In the earliest days of the camp's existence, there was no resident British medical officer, the hospital was not yet functional and whatever care was provided by the Germans was rudimentary. Even the relatively healthy might have to face the prospect of having a tooth pulled out with no anaesthetic.

The most widespread assault on the bodies of the prisoners was lice. These were arguably even more hated than the Germans. Initially picked up by many from the filthy conditions in the cattle trucks, they spread like wildfire in the overcrowded rooms of the old forts. They lodged and then hatched in the woolly seams of the men's battledress, in their blankets and in all the warm, moist areas of the body, especially in hairy areas. They drove people half mad with the itching, many men choosing to shave their heads and bodies to minimise the problem. If you scratched yourself you risked getting wounds, which made it even easier for the lice to get inside you. At least in this instance, the Germans tried to do something about it. The prisoners were forced into the showers while their clothes were quickly fumigated, but sooner or later, just when you thought you were free of them, the bastard lice would get you again.

Clothing itself was another problem. The German forces always had a demand for wool, so Allied prisoners often had their uniforms and underwear taken from them and issued with poorer-quality substitutes. When their socks wore out, all they could do was wrap their feet in rough cloth. If their British army boots fell apart, they might be issued with wooden clogs which, before their feet adjusted and toughened to the hardness of the wood, would blister and callus till walking became a torture.

Despite all this, it seems that the general level of morale among the British POWs remained fairly high. Had they known when they arrived in Torun that their captivity would last almost five more years, that may not have been the case. But despite Hitler's clean sweep across Europe and the disaster of Dunkirk, it wasn't all doom, gloom and hopelessness. There was still the lingering hope that the war might be over, if not by this Christmas, then maybe before the next. After all, the heroes of the RAF had just won the so-called Battle of Britain and the United Kingdom was, for the time being at least, saved from invasion. The parallel German strategy, the 'Blitz' on London and other major cities and ports, was now well underway and a source of huge concern, especially for prisoners who hailed from these prime targets. But the nightmare vison of the POWs – that the Swastika might fly above their home towns and villages, their loved ones interned, raped or even murdered – seemed to have receded. And what about the Yanks? Maybe something would happen that might make Roosevelt finally come and help them, just as they'd done back in 1917. Where there's life there's hope.

Of course, the prisoners in Stalag XXA were supposed to know nothing about the world beyond the south bank of the Vistula. But even from their early days, information got into the dark, damp corridors. Most of the main forts and the working camps had a wireless receiving set. These came mostly by way of Polish civilians, bartered for the desirable goods from the prisoners' Red Cross parcels (see below). Sometimes, just the necessary parts were sneaked in and the wireless assembled secretly in the camp. Occasionally, a guard could be bribed to smuggle these through the gates. Sometimes the Germans would carry out random searches for these illicit sets and all sorts of swift subterfuges would be necessary to hide them. But in this way, the German attempts to shove Hitler's propaganda down British throats was largely foiled.

Every letter the prisoners either sent or received was meticulously censored. In the Stalag XXA headquarters building, close to Fort 13, an office was manned by a large staff, mostly Polish women, responsible for checking the mail, not just of the main camp, but also of the many working camps in the surrounding region. It might be imagined that the conquered Poles, their sympathies on the side of the Allies, would do their job in a casual way. But they were carefully supervised and the batches of mail to which they were assigned were regularly changed around. So every day they ploughed through the heartfelt endearments to wives and sweethearts and the banal enquiries about Grandad's health or how little Jimmy was doing at school, searching for any sentence, going out or coming in, which might tell either party something the Third Reich did not want them to know. There was little point in the POW moaning to his wife about the state of the latrines, that the food wasn't fit for the mangiest dog or that a certain German guard was a complete sod. The censor's pen would go straight through anything that even suggested Stalag XXA was anything less than a holiday camp where the inmates were honoured and well-treated guests. Conversely, the pen would quickly obliterate any piece of good news from home about any Allied progress or reversal of fortune for the Germans.

The censors were also responsible for checking the personal parcels sent to Stalag XXA from the prisoners' loved ones. In their first months, men like Fred and Antony relied heavily on these. But as the deprivations of war began to close in back home, it became more difficult for families to get hold of everything their POW had asked for. There would be plenty of self-sacrifice in the households of Britain in order to make life a little more bearable for their boys in the camps.

But gradually a miracle occurred in the life of every single Allied POW in World War Two. This is not too melodramatic a word. The phenomenon of the Red Cross Parcel was to pull many men, both physically and emotionally, back from the brink of the misery into which so many had been staring during the early weeks and months of their imprisonment.

It is estimated that around 150,000 of these parcels were assembled every week during the five years of the war. From their country of origin, they would be sent to neutral Lisbon or to Marseilles in Vichy France, then forwarded by rail into Switzerland, where the Red Cross International Committee organised for their delivery to POW camps across Europe. The Germans, as signatories to the Geneva Convention, were forced to allow them. At first the trickle was slow, but it became more regular as the organisation improved. The parcels weren't much bigger than a shoebox, but the POWs waited for them as if for the first swallow of summer or the Second Coming. The small everyday things they had once taken for granted had now acquired the status of treasures. Getting a bar of Cadbury's Fruit & Nut was like finding the Holy Grail. A tin of fifty untipped Player's cigs was better than a night with Betty Grable.

As Fred Foster's first plea to Peggy shows, it was food and tobacco that were wanted the most, followed by the personal hygiene items, like toothpaste and razor blades, which helped you to keep some dignity. Then, as time passed and stuff wore out, clothing became a priority. A pair of boots to replace those damn clogs. New underwear to replace the disgusting old ones that were beginning to fall apart. There were books and games, too, to help fill the long, boring winter evenings.

At first, when the parcels were more sporadic, one parcel might be shared between several men, each only able to claim one item for himself. Some pilfering went on by the German guards, nor were the prisoners always allowed to keep everything they received. Tobacco and chocolate bars were fine, but some other foodstuffs were turned over to the camp cook in order to supplement the men's basic rations. The vital medical supplies went directly to those tending the sick.

Not surprisingly, the Red Cross bounty became a form of currency within the camp. In an age when a huge proportion of men smoked tobacco in one form or another, cigarettes in particular could be bartered for almost anything, even to bribe a German guard to supply an item wanted from the outside world. Tins of coffee were another valuable exchange commodity, especially later in the war, when it was increasingly hard to get in German towns.

The Red Cross parcels came from all over the world and were often distributed in a pretty random fashion. The British POW might well receive a package from the USA, Canada or even India, with some very unfamiliar foodstuffs inside. For example, an Indian parcel designed for Sikh prisoners would contain no meat of any kind.

But their value was more than just material: it was spiritual. Like the letters from home and the illicit wireless receivers, the packages represented a connection to that other world beyond the wire, underpinning the prisoners' endless need to know that they were not forgotten, abandoned in a cold and hungry limbo while everything else went on without them. And that bar of Cadbury's Fruit & Nut, the tin of corned beef or Campbell's Soup, could have magical powers, whisking you back to times and places before the world went crazy.

Despite the camaraderie and the intimate proximity of so many others, each prisoner was, in the last analysis, on his own. Alone with his memories, his hopes and his fears. Many POWs later remarked on how strongly their personal survival instinct had surfaced; a primeval reflex that had kept them going through their long ordeal. However much you might like, even care for, the people around you, they learned that you had to put yourself first. If you saw some small advantage to yourself, something that might help you to struggle on through this particular shitty day, you were a fool not to take it. Indeed, you owed it to those who loved you: your wife, your lover, your kids, your mum and dad. You *had* to get home one day. You *would* get home one day. Only then would you know happiness again.

That obsession with surviving was heightened by witnessing the fates of those who did not. Scores of men died in Stalag XXA, mostly through malnutrition or disease, but some after beatings or being shot for some misdemeanour. You had to guard against mental problems, too. Depression and anxiety, rarely admitted let alone understood or treated, were widespread. A few lost their minds entirely, one man throwing himself to his death from the roof of the fort into the dry moat below. Some people's souls simply could not breathe inside a cage.

At least the Germans usually behaved respectfully in the face of death, even when they had been responsible for it. Something of the old Prussian military ethos still lived on inside the Nazi uniforms. Prisoners who died were accorded a proper military funeral; their comrades lined up with straight backs and caps in hand, the Union Jack draped over the coffin, the Last Post trumpeted out into the cold Polish air. In his last minutes above the ground, the dead man was allowed to be a soldier again, not just a number.

For many of those with straight backs, such events were simply one more of the daily sadnesses that chimed out the hours of their captivity. Like cold, hunger and hard labour, death was just one more thing to be borne with stoicism and as much nobility as you could scrape together. For some, though, the sight of Polish earth being shovelled onto the Union Jack, until it vanished from view, was a spur. That kick up the arse they needed. Those were the men who *were* going home. No corner of a foreign field was going to be their resting place. Bugger that. They had been guests of the 'Hotel Torun' for way too long. And soon they would be checking out.

CHAPTER FOUR

They were an odd couple. At first glance anyway. The high-flying Oxford graduate and the solicitor's clerk from a small Midlands town. The son of the army officer and the son of the bricklayer. If it hadn't been for the war, it is unlikely their paths would ever have crossed.

But it seems clear that Antony Coulthard and Fred Foster saw similar qualities in one another. Both were emotionally driven by ambitious mothers, even if, in Fred's case, it was from beyond the grave. Both had a strong sense of identity; in Fred it appears to have been natural, in Antony it had evolved as he slowly came to appreciate his own prodigious gifts. Both had the precious ability to be interested in, and to reach out towards, anyone who crossed their paths.

Besides, Antony was no snob. He had refused a commission to become an officer and joined the 'other ranks'. He had stayed in the miner's cottage in depressed South Wales. On one of his student summers in Germany, he'd eagerly followed the advice of a teacher and gone out to meet the local working folk to better understand what was happening in the country. At Oxford, he may have lived to some extent in an ivory tower, but he seems always to have been aware of its dangers and to have climbed down from it as often as possible. He would certainly have much admired the likes of Fred Foster, the young man a few rungs lower on the ladder of life, who had worked so hard to pull himself higher.

If Fred found the boy wonder from the Villa Vita in any way intimidating, it's unlikely he would have shown it. If Antony started talking about Goethe, Shakespeare or Milton, Fred no doubt cheerfully admitted he knew little of such things but listened with admiration and not a little envy. Leaving school at fourteen had been a short straw and no mistake. Did he ever wonder how far he might have gone if he had had Antony's start in life? Did he ever ask him about life among the dreaming spires? Even if he didn't, Fred would have recognised that in through the fierce iron gates of Fort 13 had come somebody from whom he could learn things. And though the war had thrown his ambitions into a weird state of suspension, he would only accept that in the physical sense. Hitler would never get hold of his mind.

In short, Antony and Fred clicked. It was to be a momentous friendship for them both.

*

When Antony Coulthard arrived at Fort 13, the Nazis could hardly believe his proficiency in their language. Not just the German of the poets and writers, but of the man and woman in the street. This rare ability was the foundation on which so much was soon to depend.

Obviously, this marked him out in the eyes of the camp authorities and he was quickly selected as an interpreter. This position gave him some small privileges, including exemption from the roughest sorts of manual work. But it was a tricky job trying to smooth over the daily difficulties between his comrades and the Germans, which did not arise exclusively from the enemy side. A large body of high-spirited young prisoners and suspicious German guards ordered to enforce cast-iron regulations made for a tense and often volatile combination.

Nor was using his language skills as a means to an 'easy' life a path Antony could allow himself to take, and he would soon prove it. The distribution of the sacred Red Cross parcels was always open to corruption, by both staff and inmates. That unfortunate 'every man for himself' aspect of POW life could make it something of a 'racket', which left many prisoners seething with rage. On the first visit of the Red Cross Commissioners to Stalag XXA, Antony brought the matter to their attention and did so over the head of the Camp Commandant, through whom such complaints were supposed to be made. The authorities did not forgive him. He was stripped of his role as an interpreter and consigned for three weeks in the 'cooler'; a punishment cell located in the damp, rat-infested outer wall of the moat. Here, he was confined in almost total darkness, had to sleep on bare boards and survive on starvation rations. Afterwards, people were struck by the fact that he showed no bitterness. As he saw it, he had done the right thing and that was all that mattered.

Lance Corporal Antony Coulthard had soon stood out among hundreds of men in Fort 13. His horn-rimmed glasses and his blatant intelligence quickly earned him the nickname of 'The Professor', which would stick to him for the rest of his life. The widespread affection and respect he earned was no mean achievement. Quite unlike Fred Foster, Antony could still be reserved and diffident: the outgoing side, when he would dress up as Father Christmas at Oxford or be the life and soul of the party, only came out when you got to know him or, as he had written in that self-analytical letter to his mother before the war, when he felt himself in the company of like-minded souls who appreciated his sense of humour. But the prisoners in Stalag XXA were a motley crew of 'other ranks', most of whom, snobbish though it sounds, would not have remotely shared his tastes and interests. Had he chosen a commission and been a captive officer in, say, Colditz Castle, he would have had many more companions educated to his own level. But his principles had made that impossible and he did not regret it.

What made 'The Professor' so admired in Fort 13 seems to have been a combination of bravery and of caring for those around him. He had none of the selfishness or the cold instinct for survival that soured the characters of so many inmates. Antony Coulthard would never be involved in any 'racket', however morally justifiable it might be. And when the occasion required it, his courage impressed everyone.

On the German staff was a man known to the prisoners as 'Propaganda Joe'. This man spoke good English and his purpose was to instil despair by telling the POWs that they had lost the war and that Adolf would soon be ranting from the balcony of Buckingham Palace. At this point in 1940, the Allied situation was indeed pretty grim and the information that came through on the secret wireless sets and from new arrivals did nothing much to contradict the Germans' intolerable confidence that they would soon win World War Two. If that nightmare came true, what would happen to the inmates of Stalag XXA? Would they be kept in the Third Reich forever as a captive workforce? And if they were ever allowed back home, what would they find? An occupied Britain, squashed under the Nazi jackboot? The way of life they had known, and fought for, now gone forever?

Antony Coulthard wasn't having any of this. Though ever a realist about the war situation, he hit back, preaching to his comrades that much of what the German papers printed was biased and untrue; what we would now call 'fake news'. He squared up to 'Propaganda Joe', telling him that he meant the prisoners to hear the truth. Naturally, this did not make him popular with their captors. By now his card was definitely marked.

But this was still the dark early period of their confinement in Stalag XXA. The men had only recently lost their freedom. A few months before, they had been ordinary blokes leading normal lives; going to work, playing football or cricket on a Saturday, courting a girl. Now they were entombed in a crumbling fort in the middle of a foreign country and struggling to come to terms with their grim new reality. Most were learning to cope, but some could not and never would.

At this stage, there was still no priest present in the camp so Antony took on the job of temporary 'padre'. He may well have been an 'intellectual', instinctively questioning every so-called 'truth' with which he was presented, but his questioning clearly did not include the existence of God. Quite the contrary perhaps. His fervent admiration for the works of Goethe focused on that poet's masterpiece *Faust*, the chronicle of a man who sells his soul to the Devil. In Antony's character, intellectual rigour and simple faith seemed to be able to walk hand in hand without conflict. In the deeply testing circumstances of a prison camp, he did whatever he could to bring comfort. For the sick and the suicidal, he tried to nourish the inner strength to cling on to life. For the dying, he helped them to let go of it without fear. And for the majority who were somehow holding themselves together and getting through each day as it came, he bolstered the belief that God saw their pain and would not desert them. Among the most haunting memories of those held captive in Fort 13 would be of the man who, every Sunday evening, stood on the drawbridge over the moat and sang, in a pure, crystalline voice, 'Abide With Me'. There was never, they remembered later, a dry eye in the house.

For the work that he did in these first bleak months, a friend later wrote to Antony's mother that 'his unfailing spirit, cheerfulness and faith made him the most popular man in Stalag XXA'. Even allowing for some exaggeration, it is a striking tribute.

Though it is undeniable that his capture by the Germans was the tragedy of Antony Coulthard's life, it is arguable that it was, in a certain sense, also the making of him. In the summer of 1939, his First Class degree clutched tightly in his hand, he had stood on the brink of all possibilities. In normal times, he could have taken the train to London, walked down to Whitehall and, almost certainly, straight through the front doors of any of the great departments of state. The Foreign Office in particular would surely have lapped him up and gladly sent him to almost any embassy in Europe. But the cataclysm of war meant that his gifts were to find expression in an entirely different context. The testimonials of others make it reasonable to suggest that Antony blossomed in captivity as much, and perhaps more, as he would have done in freedom. In Stalag XXA, the potential he had to be a remarkable man was fully and wonderfully realised.

'It was always the same old "Professor,"' wrote The Reverend Lathaen, who had eventually become the official Padre. 'The unperturbed, the loose-limbed, the almost otherworldly Coulthard with that amused twinkle in his eye, peeping at you through glasses that were more than often dilapidated. At the same time, he always seemed to know what he wanted and went after it. He was as wise as a serpent and harmless as a dove.'

*

As the months passed and the Red Cross parcels began to trickle in, life in German POW camps slowly became more tolerable.

After a while, most men were able to appreciate that life, however tough, was still worth living. They were, it must be admitted, relatively safe; arguably far more so than their nearest and dearest in Britain, against whom the Luftwaffe was still directing its full force. Between the autumn of 1940 and summer of 1941, tens of thousands had been killed in the Blitzes on London, Coventry, Bristol and other major towns and cities. Had the POWs not been captured, they could have died on the retreat to Dunkirk or been sent to fight in any of the other theatres of war across the globe. There were more than a few Allied troops who envied POWs 'sitting out the war', far away from any battlefield. A notion that the prisoners were somehow 'lucky' took root among many; a notion that would have been quickly dispelled had they spent even one week in Stalag XXA.

The 200,000-odd Allied prisoners held by the Third Reich by the end of the war were, within the obvious restrictions of captivity, pretty much left alone to build and run their own societies. Apart from the requirement that the men should rise for roll call at 6am, then go off to do a day's hard work, the Germans did not impose a rigid structure on their prisoners. They provided the most basic food supplies and imposed constant surveillance, but that was about it. Within the damp walls of the forts of Torun, the attitude of the conquerors seems to have been that it was down to the prisoners to keep themselves alive. In this sense, it might almost be said that the POWs ran the camps themselves.

Next to malnutrition, boredom was the worst problem. Diversion was almost as important as food. After labouring in the fields, breaking stones in a quarry or building a road, the prospect of a monotonous evening inside the dank, poorly lit rooms of Fort 13 was deeply depressing. Conversation with the same people could quickly pall and there were perpetual small frictions engendered by frayed nerves, cramped quarters and sordid conditions. But although nothing could cure the essential grimness of their situation, plenty could be done to anaesthetise the pain.

In this context, the age-old British ability to set up a committee for absolutely anything came in very useful. Soon there would be a committee for entertainments, for the library, for physical training programmes to improve health and strength and opportunities for what we now call 'further education'. Brains' Trusts, lectures and debates were held, during one of which the motion was carried by a vote of 15 to 5 that 'the war would be over by Christmas 1942'.

As time went on, some of the entertainments reached a standard quite amazing in the circumstances. Huge amounts of time and effort went into them. As a microcosm of society, every prison camp naturally contained men with a vast array of skills that could be put to good use. There was no shortage of musicians, actors, singers and other entertainers, nor of carpenters, tailors, electricians and so on. As they used to say in corny old Hollywood musicals, 'Let's do the show right here!'

Spaces were found in which to create a makeshift theatre. In Fort 13, the 'Little Theatre' was described as 'a little gem of cardboard and distemper'. There were proper curtains, footlights and printed programmes. Scenery was painted on Red Cross food boxes, costumes created from spare material by the clever fingers of the tailors. Wigs could be made out of the string from parcels. Ingenuity knew no limits. One of Fred and Antony's close comrades was a young actor and entertainer called Sam Kydd,* who was a driving force behind, and leading light in, many of the productions. The choices were almost always light; laughter was the best medicine for an audience of prisoners. Variety shows were the staple fare – comedy and songs – but full-length plays were produced, too. Classic farces like *Rookery Nook*, West End hits such as *George & Margaret*, even Oscar Wilde's *The Importance of Being Earnest* and Gilbert & Sullivan's *Mikado*. At least once though, they strayed into more serious territory with R.C. Sherriff's famous play about the Great War, *Journey's End*. Female roles were taken by the younger, more willowy men who would look better in a frock than some big hairy sergeant with three days' stubble. No doubt the ribaldry the 'girls' endured is unprintable.

For the variety shows, the 'turns' were accompanied by members of the camp orchestra, which also gave classical concerts of its own. The Fort 13 orchestra had evolved in less than a year from a pianist and violinist to eleven players. Even an experienced orchestral conductor was found. One typical programme included Schubert's *Unfinished Symphony* and the overtures to *Hansel & Gretel* and *Die Fledermaus*. Larger instruments like pianos and double basses were tracked down in the local area. Much of the rest was sent through by the inexhaustible efforts of the Red Cross or the Prisoners of War department in London. They not only sent violins, clarinets, flutes and piano accordions, but also vocal scores and sheet music for the orchestral parts of popular classics, as well as 'self-tutor' manuals for banjos and ukeleles for anyone who fancied himself as the next George Formby.

Other camps were even better served. One had an orchestra of no fewer than fifty musicians. Yet another boasted a fifteen-piece dance band and specialised in big musicals like *The Desert Song* and *The Wizard*

* Sam Kydd (1915-1982) was imprisoned in various POW camps for nearly five years. He wrote a colourful account of his experiences in *For You The War Is Over* (Futura 1974), which is both tragic and very funny. After the war, he became an acclaimed character actor in over 200 films including *I'm All Right Jack*, *Reach for the Sky*, *The Killing of Sister George* and *Too Late the Hero*. He was equally famous on television, working with stars such as Tony Hancock and Eric Sykes, but is perhaps best remembered for the 1960s series *Crane* and its spin-off *Orlando*, which was specially written for him, and as a recurring character in *Coronation Street* playing Mike Baldwin's father. After their years in Stalag XXA, Sam Kydd and Fred Foster remained lifelong friends.

of Oz. The bandsmen's uniforms, their music stands and stage decorations were all made from Red Cross boxes and sheeting. This band was even allowed to make a short tour of the outlying working parties, as if they were the Glenn Miller Orchestra itself. The bigger shows would sometimes run for a week or more so that everyone in Stalag XXA and the outlying working camps had the chance to see them. A production might easily play to nearly ten thousand or more.

It is remarkable to what degree the Germans went along with all this and even encouraged it. No doubt they realised the value of it: releasing tensions, improving morale and making their own daily job just a little bit easier. The programme for one show gratefully acknowledges the assistance given by the German staff, where the Commandant had helped the performers obtain props, make-up and women's dresses. Musicians were even allowed under guard into nearby towns to buy 'spare parts' for their instruments. At the performances, the German Commandant and his senior staff would sit in the front row and dutifully applaud, even if they didn't always know quite what was going on. The humour of *Rookery Nook* probably passed them by. In a strange way, it must have seemed almost civilised, this coming together of victors and vanquished in the pursuit of 'art'. Bizarre, then, to remember that just a mile of two away in the Russian camp, men were being starved, beaten and murdered on a regular basis.

Sport was another obvious 'safety valve'. There were boxing matches, games of rugby and cricket and, above all, football. In time, one camp even had a full-sized pitch. Certainly in the early years, these activities were constricted somewhat by the diminished physical strength of many of the players: it was difficult to be a decent prop forward when you'd been labouring hard all week and your weight had sunk to half of what it had been before.

For those for whom sport was too strenuous, gardening was a popular alternative. The Red Cross sent out thousands of seed packets and small gardening implements to camps across Europe. To supplement their basic rations and the treats in the Red Cross parcels, tomatoes, lettuces, cabbages and potatoes were all grown to help the

POWs keep healthy. But flowers mattered too, and many a grim brick wall was softened with a climbing rose and a scrubby patch of ground turned into a bed of tulips and daffodils.

Arguably, however, books were the most treasured resource and not just for the likes of Antony Coulthard. Men who had never been great readers soon discovered there was no better escape than a good story. Especially perhaps if it vividly described the landscape, characters and way of life back home.

'Books are food and drink to me,' one prisoner wrote to the Red Cross, which had now set up an educational books section based in the Bodleian Library in Oxford. But there was no intellectual snobbery and it tried to cater to all tastes; from the lightest novels to the heaviest literature. In time, however, many men who had never tried anything more serious than P.G. Wodehouse or John Buchan had begun to tackle Thomas Hardy, Anthony Trollope, the Brontes and even Jane Austen. Books were also sent by the prisoners' families. Fred Foster loved Dickens and wrote to Peggy asking her to send a copy of *David Copperfield*, one of his favourite novels. Perhaps the roller-coaster life of its eponymous hero reflected the tumult of his own recent experience. In such ways, camp libraries often grew steadily to contain several thousand volumes. But the Germans imposed a degree of censorship. No Jewish authors were allowed. Nor were Secret Service stories or even, incredibly, tales about scouting, in case these gave prisoners ideas on means of escape. Left-leaning authors like George Bernard Shaw, H.G. Wells and J.B Priestley were banned, too.

The library also became the focus for those who wanted to study for careers to take up on their hoped-for return to civilian life. Gradually, British colleges began to supply POWs with study courses and to let them sit examinations to gain qualifications. Again, the aim was to help as broad a range of prisoners as possible. The spectrum of available subjects went from languages, banking, medicine and law to engineering, land agency, hospital administration and many other more mundane trades. Fred Foster was one of this number, managing to pick up where he had left off in his climb up the ladder. It seems extraordinary now that a structure existed for POWs in Germany to study for British academic qualifications, but that was the case. It must have seemed a weirdly contrasting set of circumstances. the Third Reich would do its best to help you get on in life, but it would also be quite prepared to shoot you dead if you tried to climb through the wire.

Antony Coulthard, once relieved of his temporary duties as 'padre', naturally started up a language school. In the circumstances, German was the obvious choice for most students. If, God forbid, the Nazis did conquer the world, it might be useful to speak the bastards' lingo. He was a strict teacher; expecting regular attendance and hard work, quite prepared to chastise somebody senior to him if he felt they were swinging the lead. Conversely, he would have noticed that Fred Foster was one of his most conscientious students, albeit not one of the best. Fred's strong East Midlands accent was a handicap, making his pronunciation of German a bizarre listening experience.

If Antony ever wondered what made the affable sergeant from Newark refuse to give up, he would soon find out.

CHAPTER FIVE

I t seems likely that Sergeant Fred Foster of the 8th Sherwood Foresters decided to escape from Stalag XXA at pretty much the exact moment he had walked through its gates.

Instead of being traumatised by the Battle of Tretten Gorge, by the sight of Lt Esam and other comrades shot dead or blown to bits, Fred appears to have been mobilised into a fierce determination to survive. He had already seen his mother Ethel die young and now Jack Esam and the rest. Perhaps the fragility and preciousness of life had come home to him for the first time in his twenty-five years.

Only three weeks after he'd arrived at Torun in May 1940, and while he'd still not yet received any message from her in return, Fred wrote to Peggy with what must have seemed a slightly odd request.

'Can you send me a primary course in German? I would like to learn the language thoroughly while I am here,' he asked. 'Also a round biscuit tin of dripping. Always send plenty of that.'

Dripping would have been simple for Peggy to find, but tracking down German course books must have been a bit trickier in a town like Barnard Castle. It seems that Fred didn't wait for either item because just two weeks later he writes that his German speech is coming along well, presumably by trying to engage his guards in basic conversation.

For every prisoner of war, it was regarded as an almost sacred duty to attempt escape. To this way of thinking, every successful escape was part of the war effort. A small but symbolic punch on the nose for Adolf and his ghastly ideology. No doubt that was indeed the prime motivation for many escapees. For most, however, it was a much more human one. Just getting home to those you loved.

Fred Foster was emphatically in the second category. All he really wanted was to see Peggy and hold her in his arms again. Nearly eighty years on, reading their letters makes the intensity of his passion achingly clear. His yearning for her leaps off the pages. The extrovert Fred, with a penchant for blue, barrack-room humour, almost turns into a romantic poet, pouring out his feelings of adoration without restraint. The beautiful girl on the train had come into his life out of nowhere. Here was his soulmate. Here was the map of his future in total clarity. A long straight road to happiness. A home of their own. A crop of kids. Working hard, getting on in his career, bettering himself as his mother had so much wanted for him. Then came war.

When he had parted from Peggy, he had known her for only five months, been married for just five weeks. Damn the war, damn Hitler. People around him kept up the constant bleat that it'd be over by Christmas, but he had stopped believing it. They were whistling in the dark, he thought. His new chum 'The Professor', usually so cheerful, didn't seem too optimistic about it either. Whatever happened, Fred Foster wasn't going to lie back on his thin, hard mattress and wait patiently for it to happen.

'My darling, every feature of yours I am carrying in my head. Even in the heat of battle when it seemed I should be certain to bid *au revoir* to you, I thought to myself, "This is how Peggy would be proud to have you go out." But God willed that our short happiness was not to end then dear and that is why I thank Him every night.'

Eventually Peggy's first letters reached him in one joyful batch and their contact became more regular. Over the summer and autumn of 1940, he reassured his wife that he was in good health and contented. The Germans are treating us well enough, he reported. One wonders how much of this was true and not merely to comfort the folks back home. He even claimed to be fatter than when he left England, an assertion which, given the near-starvation rations the prisoners were suffering before the Red Cross parcels began to kick in, can hardly have been true.

These white lies were necessary. It is clear from the letters that Peggy was also finding it hard not to be despondent and hopeless. It was difficult for her to see other people's husbands and sweethearts come home on leave and stroll hand in hand along the streets of Barnard Castle. These men may have been in more imminent danger than Fred now was, but at least they came home from time to time. How unlucky she and Fred had been. She had found the man she loved only to have him snatched away again in no time. And for how long? It was all so unfair. She was only twenty after all, not yet hardened against the vicissitudes of life. At one point, she told him she could no longer write him a letter every single day as he did to her. Possibly, that daily ritual of finding something cheerful to say was having the very opposite effect. Perhaps she just needed some days when she could try to blot their predicament out of her mind and think of something else, anything else.

No doubt it was his growing awareness of her misery that spurred his intention to escape. He may also have been aware of the wives and girlfriends of his comrades who were going through the same emotions. Many prisoners received 'Dear John' letters, either from the women themselves or from their own families, that heralded the end of a marriage or a romance. The girl who couldn't wait any longer. The wife, depressed and frustrated, who'd sought comfort somewhere else and maybe got herself into trouble. However rock-sure Fred was of his new bride's devotion, he'd have been superhuman if such things hadn't sent a shudder through him. Time and time again, the same hint now began to be dropped through all Fred's letters home.

'Don't worry, I'll be back for our anniversary,' he wrote. 'Nothing shall ever take me away from you again. The schemes I devolve in the long night hours...'

If the censors noticed anything suspicious in these lines, they must have regarded it as harmless wishful thinking.

'Remember sweet,' he told his wife, 'be it six months or five years, I am coming back to you. I, too, often imagine you sitting on a station waiting for me.'

He had no intention, however, that she would have to sit there for five years.

*

We do not, as already mentioned, know if Antony Coulthard had left a sweetheart behind when he had sailed so eagerly to his first posting to Brittany. Or even just somebody of whom, like the girl in the photograph taken on the bridge, he had vague hopes for the future. Somebody who, even today, may still have a tranche of letters from him just like those Fred was writing to Peggy.

What we do know from his letters home to the Villa Vita is how much he missed the places that had formed the backdrop to his young life so far. In the rare moments of solitude it was possible to find in this crowded, regimented place, he let his mind return to them.

'There are some lovely quiet spots on the roof of this fort where one can sit till sundown and forget for a moment that one is a prisoner,' he wrote. 'But it is no compensation for the sea and the forests and hills. In a sunset fantasy, I let my fancy wander onto the towers of London, Southampton Water, the dreaming spires of Oxford and finally, as twilight fell, follow the Thames to its trickling source among the Cotswolds.'

He remembered, too, the summer holidays with his sisters at the home of his grandmother in the Channel Islands.

'Sometimes as I sit on a jutting wing of the fort, especially if a fresh wind is swaying the treetops, I try to imagine I am on the cliffs in Guernsey, watching the foam break on the shore. Though I am soon called back to reality by the sight of a sentry patrolling the ramparts.'

It must have been painful to remember that those cliffs, that sea and those islands were now occupied by the Germans. But sentries or not, it was still possible for him to snatch odd moments of beauty.

Chapter Five

'Hidden from sight by the bushes, I can hear a gramophone playing Schubert's lovely *Rosamunde Interlude* and Haydn's *Surprise Symphony*.'

German composers both. One wonders whether the gramophone was being played by a prisoner or a guard. Antony may have hoped it was the latter, to prove that not everything in the spirit of the Germany he had loved had been entirely trampled under the jackboot.

Antony had never concealed from any of his comrades his resolve to make an escape attempt. Those who did not know him well must have thought the slight young man in the glasses an unlikely candidate for such an escapade. Those who knew him better, who had heard how he had boldly driven his motorcycle straight towards the enemy in Amiens, would not have agreed. If anyone had both the brains and the guts needed to get out of there, it was 'The Professor'.

But there were strict procedures to be followed and many aspects to be considered. Among those was the question of whether you made your attempt alone or with somebody else.

For Antony Coulthard, that question was answered one evening in early 1941 when his friend Sergeant Fred Foster took him quietly aside and suggested they might go through the wire together. He had, Fred whispered, the outline of a plan. Antony agreed on the spot.

*

The plan they developed was breathtaking in its danger and its sheer bloody cheek.

For any prisoner thinking of waving goodbye to Stalag XXA, there was one obvious route home. Assuming he managed to get through the wire, he would head for the Polish port of Gdansk on the Baltic coast, no more than eighty miles north of Torun, though, unless he was lucky, it would probably be on foot. There, he would somehow get himself on board a ship to neutral Sweden. The trouble was that this obvious route was just as obvious to the Germans. That was why they had established a network of informers at the docks, often their Italian allies, to report on any suspicious men trying to get a passage across the Baltic from a friendly captain. Despite this, there had been, and would be in the future, a fair number of successful escapes this way, mostly by men in the outlying working parties away from the main camp.

Another possible strategy was to go east towards Russia with the help of the Polish resistance. Half of the thirty or so successful escapes from Stalag XXA during the war were made this way, again mostly by men from the working camps where security was lighter than in the main forts. But it was a dubious choice. The escapees' welcome in Russia was often cold and some were even maltreated and sent on trains to Siberia to endure a long wait before eventual repatriation.

Antony Coulthard and Fred Foster decided on a different road to freedom. Their plan was to take a train from Torun station and, in stages, ride into Germany itself, all the way across it into neutral Switzerland. This involved a journey of no less than nine hundred miles, though there would at least be no walking. Wearing civilian clothing, they would pose as two businessmen travelling to Switzerland. It was that simple and that complicated. As opposed to the much shorter route to Gdansk, such an option would expose them for far longer to both enemy forces and an enemy population. But the rationale was that, once the Germans had discovered their escape, they would be far less likely to search for them on the Swiss route than on the Baltic one. It was a clever strategy, but a high-risk one. They would be heading straight into the heart of the Third Reich, straight into the lion's den.

Success or failure would depend entirely on one thing: their ability to pass themselves off as native German speakers. The weight of this rested largely on Antony, whose fluency would be their passport to freedom. The serious challenge was to get Fred's skills up to a level where he could just about pass muster during the time required. It would be, as Fred put it, 'one big bluff'.

It was bold, daring and, let's face it, exciting. It would have appealed strongly to the risk-taking side of Antony's character. What a coup, he must have thought, if they could pull it off. How wonderful to cock such a snook at Adolf and his crew. How stylish just to buy a ticket and coolly ride out of Germany and on a train infinitely more salubrious than the nightmarish cattle-truck in which he had arrived. What a great yarn for his Oxford chums after the war. Something to tell the grandchildren when he was old and grey.

Fred Foster no doubt felt the same. One day soon, in the pubs of Newark, Harry Foster might be proudly telling people how his lad Fred had outwitted those Nazi bastards. And Harry's mates would nod, buy another round and raise their glasses to a new local hero.

It is not clear, nor does it much matter, which of them came up with the final plan for their escape. Both were determined to get out of Stalag XXA and different ideas had been percolating in both their heads for some time before Fred approached Antony. But it seems certain that Fred, for several months at least, had been laying some firm foundations for an escape, even if he had not yet worked out the structure of the enterprise.

Given the serious deprivations still existing in Stalag XXA at that time, it is remarkable that a camp newspaper had been launched almost from the very beginning. There were quite a few benefits attached to working on *Prisoners' Pie,* but Fred seems to have been most interested in one in particular. It would give him access to a typewriter. A typewriter with a German keyboard. A necessity for forging the documents vital to any escape attempt.

This meant somehow getting onto the staff that put the magazine together. Only weeks after he'd first arrived at Stalag XXA, Fred Foster had achieved this by a bold and risky strategy.

The current editor had been one Sergeant Chappell, a man widely suspected of being a German collaborator; one of those despicable, but rather pathetic, souls who had decided to hitch themselves to Hitler's triumphant wagon. Sadly, it has to be admitted here that there existed a particular breed of NCOs in prisoner of war camps for whom the 'other ranks' felt a disrespect that sometimes bordered on hatred. This derived from the conviction, often justified, that these NCOs, whilst falling short of active collaboration, were greedy and selfish, wangling themselves the 'cushy' jobs, filching the best stuff from the Red Cross parcels and far too chummy with the camp authorities.

'They were guilty in many, many cases of cheating the soldiers to whom they were supposed to set an example,' Sam Kydd later wrote about those in the cookhouse. 'They became so suspect at cutting the bread – so vital to starving men – that it had to be seen to be done in the open, fairly and honestly. The POW [identity] disc was exactly a fifth of a loaf in width and this became the standard of measurement when five men shared a loaf. The rations they had to play with were meagre for seven hundred men, but they either didn't seem to get the hang of it or there was a fiddle going on. It was rumoured that they were having pork chops and chips every evening in the cookhouse.'

But it seems that Sergeant Chappell's misdemeanours went far beyond the dishonest slicing of a loaf. Fred Foster had sneaked a look at a letter from Chappell to the Camp Commandant asking to start a prisoners' magazine, in which he assured the Commandant that he was aware of the duties of an editor under the Third Reich and would conform to the standards laid down by Germany. Fred took this evidence to RSM Sivers, the senior British NCO in the camp, who agreed that Chappell must somehow be got rid of. But how?

Calmly and expertly, Fred set about framing Chappell. *Prisoners' Pie* was sold at 10 *pfennigs* per copy, a small charge that covered the cost of the printing by a company in the centre of Torun. Chappell kept these 'takings' in a box. Fred then stole one hundred marks from this box and reported the theft to the German quartermaster, who was in charge of ordering the paper and ink, saying that Chappell was pocketing the takings. To prove it, he showed him the accounts and the now-depleted contents of the box. The German quartermaster agreed that Chappell must be sacked, but asked who would now take over as editor. With a token show of reluctance, Fred then agreed to do it. And Bob's your uncle; the vital typewriter was now his.

'My literary attainments were rather limited,' Fred wrote later, 'but I knew I could quite easily put something together: the sports reports, items of interest extracted from letters from home and articles or short stories written by the prisoners themselves.'

Chapter Five

Fred renamed the magazine *The New Prisoners' Pie* and turned it into a far better publication than before, making it a much stronger link with home for the lads than it had ever been when in the hands of a German collaborator.*

The magazine's office was in the headquarters of Stalag XXA, the overall administration centre for all the forts, the nearby camps and the scattered working parties. This was in a modern, three-storey building on a side road between Fort 13 and the south bank of the Vistula. It was also the location of the censor's office and the depot for the Red Cross parcel deliveries. Though the various departments were headed by German officers, they were partly staffed by Polish civilians, often women, and the dogsbody jobs were filled by the POWs themselves, some of whom, like Sam Kydd, took advantage of their proximity to the opposite sex.

The Germans had located the magazine offices close to the censors, so that they could keep a sharp eye on what was being published. Despite this, Fred was proud that he managed to circulate several of Churchill's speeches, delivered during Britain's darkest hours. Listening secretly on the underground radio, he had taken them down in shorthand then typed them up.

'We shall fight on the beaches... We shall never surrender.'

It was exactly what the prisoners of Stalag XXA, stuck in the limbo of their captivity, needed to hear. They needed to know that the fight was still going on and that their homeland, however battered and bruised, was still undefeated and waiting for them to return.

Eventually, Fred made contact with a member of the Polish underground, a man named Andreas. He had been a sergeant-major in the Polish Army but now, his country under Nazi occupation, he worked in the tobacco stores at Stalag HQ, responsible for the storage and distribution of the trash-tobacco the POWs had to tolerate as being better than nothing. Fred would loiter in the corridor outside the stores till the

---

* Soon afterwards, Sergeant Chappell left Stalag XXA and went to Berlin to join the Britisches Freikorps, a unit of the Waffen SS manned by British traitors, where he produced a magazine distributed to the POW camps, which was essentially a mouthpiece for German propaganda. After the war, he was tried by court martial and imprisoned for ten years.

coast was clear, then nip in and give Andreas the latest BBC news from the secret wireless sets in exchange for local information. In time, when trust between them had been built up, it was arranged that, in exchange for Red Cross parcels, the Polish underground would supply civilian clothing necessary for any escape.

With Fred increasingly confident that getting through the wire was a serious possibility, he had then spoken to Antony Coulthard. He must have thanked his lucky stars that Antony had walked through the gates of Fort 13. It had been clear to him at once that 'The Professor' was highly intelligent and imaginative, not to mention those faultless language skills, while Fred brought a forensic eye for detail, a determined work ethic and a gutsy, imperturbable character. The combination was perfect and they both knew it.

They could not, however, simply stroll off of their own volition. They may have been prisoners but they were still British soldiers with wages being paid to their families back home. And they were still subject to military discipline. So each POW camp had an Escape Committee whose permission was required to make your attempt. Every breakout, whether a success or a failure, could have harsh repercussions on everyone else; restrictions would be imposed and comforts removed as punishment. Besides, you really needed its help with the practicalities: attempts that failed were always those that were too hasty and badly planned.

So Coulthard and Foster took their plan to the Escape Committee for approval. This committee was, by necessity, a highly discreet and indeed nebulous body. It didn't 'sit' formally like a judge and jury or a board of directors. The necessary conversations were held in quiet corners of the camp in the fields during work, or after lights out.

At its head was RSM Sivers. There was also Sergeant Granger, the 'Man of Confidence', another senior NCO whose oddly named role was daily liaison with the German staff. 'The Man of Confidence' was a sort of Ombudsman, receiving complaints from both directions, trying to find resolutions and generally keeping the lid on what could sometimes be a fractious atmosphere. Others on the committee were non-combatants such as Captain Bob Moody, the Medical Officer from New Zealand and the Reverend Lathaen, the Padre, whose official positions made it easier for them to get both outside information and materials to support the escape attempts. Important intelligence, such as details of enemy activities in the local area, was often gleaned from the civilian Poles coming to work in Stalag XXA or from the working parties whose men were in closer contact with the local population than those based in the main forts.

No doubt the eyebrows of the Escape Committee were sharply raised at Foster and Coulthard's idea. By train all the way across Germany itself? Surrounded by the enemy for every second of the journey? Were they joking? Nobody had ever tried such a thing before. Bloody hell, these two had guts if nothing else. Approval was given. This meant that they could immediately access a support network of different skills within the camp to help them achieve their goal.

Given Fred's yearning to get home to Peggy and Antony's simple determination to get out of there, it might seem surprising that well over a year would pass between this point and the escape itself. But to both their credits, wisdom had prevailed. If they were going to do it, they had to do it right. Preparation was everything. And since their success might depend on Fred's ability to speak German, even passably well, it was going to take some time.

As well as the regular German classes with other prisoners, Fred now began intensive one-to-one tutorials with Antony. It was hard work for them both, but especially for Fred, the boy who'd left school at fourteen. German is an easy language in the sense that it is pronounced more or less as it is spelt, but is also difficult as many nouns are polysyllabic and some parts of verbs go at the beginning of a sentence and others at the very end. Fred clearly struggled, but never gave up.

'Oh what a wearying job it turned out to be,' he said. 'Every single evening for fifteen months, I did three hours on my German and if I got a little bit sick of it all at times, Tony made me stick to it until eventually I spoke pretty well perfect German.'

The others around them, as they huddled together in a corner with their course books, must have suspected something was going on, but wouldn't have asked any questions. Though it was supposedly their duty to attempt escape, there were plenty who didn't wish to do so. Some of those who successfully escaped later spoke of active discouragement from certain quarters within the camp hierarchy, even alleging that a couple of attempts had been betrayed to the Germans. More importantly, as conditions in the POW camps improved due to the Red Cross, the decision to 'sit it out' became more widespread. If you'd managed to adjust to being a captive, had stayed passably healthy and kept serious depression at bay, then the best way of making sure you saw your wife and kids again was to stay put and keep your head down. Was getting out of Stalag XXA really worth the risk of a bullet in the back as you stumbled through the wire? Was there really much point in undertaking a night-mare journey across occupied Poland with a high chance of simply being recaptured and sent back again? Many thought not.

But there were always those who would never adjust to imprison-ment. Those for whom growing roses and tomatoes or taking part in a jolly production of *The Wizard of Oz* could never remotely compensate for the loss of their freedom. Writing to Peggy, Fred had a name for the bouts of depression that would sometimes overwhelm his usual optimis-tic nature.

'I want you to disregard entirely the letter I sent a short time ago. I must confess that, say, once every three months, that horrible "barbed wire fever" comes over one and the best thing to do then is not to say a word or write a letter until it lifts.'

On the second anniversary of his capture, he was particularly down, expressing the nagging fear of many POWs that absence might not necessarily make the hearts of their loved ones grow fonder.

'Tell me dear heart, tell me honestly, am I something like you wanted for a husband? Tell me what failings you notice in me and, before I come home, I will try to correct them. You see I happen to love you so very much that I want to make myself as near perfect as possible in your eyes.'

Chapter Five

Clearly the only cure for this 'barbed wire fever' was escape. The compulsion to achieve it was just something in the psyche. Either you felt it or you didn't. Antony and Fred were two of those who did. Neither was the sort to just sit back and settle for whatever circumstances came his way. They had been born free men; they must be free men again.

CHAPTER SIX

E scaping from a POW camp was a jigsaw that had to be painstakingly put together. Teaching Fred to speak fluent German was the
most important part of their plan, but was by no means the only
one.

Getting civilian clothing for the journey was the next big piece.
Fred's Polish friend Andreas had warned him that getting two business
suits would be a long job. They started to pay him by instalments of the
goodies from their Red Cross parcels and had themselves measured up
by an inmate who was a tailor. These measurements, taken with pieces
of string, were smuggled by Andreas to a Polish tailor on the outside
who eventually delivered two perfectly-fitting suits, made from bales of
pre-war cloth that had been hidden away from the Germans at the
time of the occupation. He also provided shirts, ties and shoes. Another
Polish helper, in exchange for half a pound of tea, made two brand new
trilby hats.

All these escape clothes were somehow smuggled into the headquarters building of Stalag XXA. On their arrival, Fred would go to the
lavatory in the fort and put on the item under his battledress. He would
then be marched down to the Stalag HQ, his place of work, where he
waited for an opportunity to slip across to the adjacent stable block
where the German officers' horses were kept. There the item was
removed and handed over to the POWs who worked there as grooms.

The grooms then added it to the wardrobe of escape clothes now being stored in two bags hidden deep inside piles of straw. No doubt praying that no horsey smells would cling to them.

The Escape Committee began to collect as much information as they could about the German/Swiss frontier. Like the clothing, this, too, was something of a slow process. Being so far away, and a previously untried route by anyone in Stalag XXA, nobody knew anything very much about the area. All they could come up with was a pathetic small-scale map torn out of an old geography book.

Vitally, Antony and Fred had to find out more about their departure point, the train station at Torun. Although members of working parties who had laboured there briefed them as well as possible, they needed to know more. Above all, a timetable was required. Not much point in getting through the wire and reaching the station if they then sat on their hands on the platform waiting for any old train that might puff their way and going to heaven knows where. A serious recce was required, but how?

The answer was kindly provided by the Germans themselves. Among their few considerate gestures to their captives was a mobile film unit, which toured the camps showing very old movies on an equally old projector. Its circuit covered about two hundred miles and needed POW help to carry the apparatus. Wangling yourself onto this team was considered a nice break from the dull old routine and a great way of seeing chums in other camps, but Fred Foster had a far more serious agenda. The Escape Committee managed to get his name to the top of the list and off he went in the company of Sam Kydd. Their little tour delivered a lot of useful information about the roads surrounding the camp. On reaching Torun station, Fred performed a small mental miracle by memorising the timetable, the cost of the tickets and the relevant passes required to move from one place to another. But their trip ended abruptly when Fred and Sam, carrying heavy, unwieldly equipment, refused to obey the German rule of prisoners walking in the gutter when passing through towns. They insisted on walking on the pavement for safety reasons and after nearly braining two civilians with the long legs of a camera tripod, the guards lost their cool and sent them straight back to Fort 13. But by now, Fred had the information he had set out to get.

The next major task was to get hold of the German identification card, the *Ausweis*, in order to forge copies of it. At least half a dozen paths were explored but the German guards they risked bribing were all too scared of being found out, even for the temptation of chocolate and coffee from the Red Cross parcels. But one day Fred was talking to a man called Mac who had come into the fort from a working party in the nearby town of Schneidemuhle in order to buy supplies from the canteen. Fred knew Mac quite well and confided their difficulty in getting a sight of a pass. The working party to which Mac belonged was labouring for Siemens, one of the biggest industrial concerns in Germany. He said he could help and was as good as his word. A week later, early in the morning, Mac came back to Fort 13 with an *Ausweis* that he had stolen from the jacket of a German worker, hung up all day while he did a strenuous job in the warm weather.

The pass would have to be back in the jacket by five o'clock when the German finished his work and would reach for his jacket to go home. There was no time to lose. Fred got the pass straight to a fellow inmate called Jimmy Woolcock, who had been an artist in civilian life. Jimmy sketched a quick facsimile and the original was back in the German's jacket by half past three and none the wiser. From this rough sketch, Jimmy created two forgeries in less than a week. They were little masterpieces. Fred and Antony felt sure that nobody would ever spot that they were fakes.

Now they needed the government stamps with which most German passes were usually covered: Nazi stamps with the eagle and swastika, police stamps, work stamps, local stamps. The master craftsmen of Stalag XXA tried every which way to duplicate the necessary stamping apparatus. First they attempted to find some linoleum but could not do so. Then they experimented with wood blocks but these could not provide enough detail. Finally, in desperation, they turned to India rubbers. These worked far better and for weeks Jimmy and Fred industriously carved away at the rubbers with razor blades until they produced something like the stamps they needed.

Next, a photograph had to be affixed to each pass. Since Antony and Fred's bespoke suits had not yet been delivered, they borrowed a couple of ill-fitting jackets from the camp theatre's costume store and posed for the POW photographer's secret underground camera.

Beyond the *Ausweis* stolen from the jacket pocket, Mac from Schneidemuhle had blessed them with another priceless gift. Half a dozen blank Siemens letter headings, filched from a drawer during sweeping out. On one of these, Fred now typed a letter of permission for the bearers to visit any Siemens factory anywhere in occupied Europe or Switzerland. Following the same procedure used with the stamps, he signed the letter with the managing director's signature, copied from that of the Camp Commandant, which was easily available, being at the foot of all notices posted for the attention of the prisoners.

Despite Fred having memorised the train timetable at Torun station, they still were not clear how long the journey to the Swiss frontier might take. It would be a journey of leaps and bounds, changing trains several times, dealing with each set of circumstances as they arose. Food was therefore a consideration. They could take a little with them, but there were two factors to be considered. Firstly, it would have to be British food from the Red Cross parcels and to be seen eating it might attract suspicion. Secondly, if they had been stopped and searched at any point, the discovery of these supplies would have given the game away. Fred and Antony then discovered that special traveller's ration coupons were necessary to buy snacks at railway stations and hotels. Their Polish contacts could not help this time and they had to take the chance on bribing a German guard. The guard must have known exactly what these were for. It was a huge gamble, which could have sent then straight to the 'cooler' or even worse but, once again, it paid off.

And so, day by day, week by week, the pieces of the jigsaw slotted into place. By mid June 1942, there was still one that didn't fit perfectly. It was an important piece, too. Fred Foster's German. During those

fifteen months of blood, sweat and tears, he had become highly profi-
cient in both vocabulary and grammar. But, despite Antony's best
efforts, his accent was still poor. He simply could not suppress his
strong Nottinghamshire vowels. Any native German hearing Fred
speak might do a double take and wonder where on earth he came
from. So it was decided that Fred would play the part of Dr Benecz, a
German-speaking Hungarian, which might help explain his strange
accent. They would just have to pray that any German he spoke to had
never gone on holiday to Budapest. Antony would be re-christened as
Dr Neumann, a native German. It was still a risky business, but neither
Fred Foster nor Antony Coulthard was afraid of risks. They had come
this far, worked so hard to get everything just right, that the idea of
aborting the escape now was anathema.

But then, just as they were ready to go, other hurdles rose up in their
path.

The very day after they had finalised their arrangements, Fred
decided to play a game of handball. Twisting his knee awkwardly, his
leg swelled up to twice its normal size. Instead of going through the
wire towards freedom, he spent the next six weeks in the camp hospital.
In normal circumstances, this would have been welcomed as a restful
holiday, but now it was a bitter blow. Luckily the leg mended well and
the patient moved quickly from bed rest onto crutches, then to a stick.
All the time he was going over the details of the escape plan in his head,
making sure nothing had been forgotten. At the end of July, he came
out of hospital and he and Antony once more prepared themselves for
the great day. It was to be 4 August 1942.

Then misfortune struck again. On the evening of 2 August,
Squadron Leader Brian Paddon was brought into Fort 13. A whole
year previously, Paddon had been imprisoned in Fort 15, used as a
punishment facility for officers from other camps, and here he had
struck a German Sergeant Major. Though it had taken them a long
time to frame the charges and bring him to trial, the Germans regarded
this as a major offence: at the very least Paddon was likely to get five or
ten years' hard labour; at worst, he might well be executed.

For some reason, Paddon had not been thrust into the 'hole in the wall' cell in which Antony had once spent three weeks, but had been allowed to spend the night with the British medical staff who were always officers and therefore of Paddon's 'status'. His trial was scheduled for ten o'clock the next morning, 3 August. Acutely aware of the possible outcome, Paddon asked RSM Sivers, head of the Escape Committee, to help get him out of Fort 13 that very night.

RSM Sivers then went to Antony and Fred and asked them to delay their own attempt in order to let Paddon go first. As this was possibly a matter of life and death, they naturally agreed. An emergency escape plan was now needed, to which Fred and Antony contributed their now detailed knowledge of the surrounding area. The summer night was short and at six o'clock, Squadron Leader Paddon walked out of Fort 13 with an early-morning working party, dressed as one of 'the boys'. When they reached the work site, Paddon simply melted off into the countryside and took his chances.

Back at the fort, a heavily armed guard arrived to take Paddon to his trial. In the room where he had supposedly slept, only the officers' batman was to be found. He told them Paddon must be on the lavatory or strolling on the grassy area up on the roof. The guards tramped down to the foul-smelling latrines, where they searched every cubicle in vain. The rest of the building was searched high and low. As planned, the prisoners told the guards they'd just seen Paddon 'going through there' or that they had 'spoken to him a few minutes ago'. A roll call was immediately organised, but no sign of Paddon. By now the Germans were hopping mad.

Over at the courtroom, all the bigwigs were rolling up in flashy cars, clicking their heels and 'heiling Hitler' twenty to the dozen. There was a general from Leipzig, colonels from all around, plus civilian solicitors and many others. It seems that a big show trial had been planned, which probably meant that Paddon hadn't stood a chance. Somewhere round the back, the firing squad was probably polishing its rifles.

When the bigwigs were ready to start, an orderly was sent to bring in the prisoner. When he returned with the news that Paddon was missing, all hell broke loose. Every poor guard deemed potentially responsible was put under arrest. The fleet of flashy cars roared off to Fort 13 where the bigwigs themselves, mad as hell, conducted a search, actually going to the latrines and kicking open doors. It must have been quite a sight. All day long, the fort was turned upside down with the British POWs repeating their 'I thought I saw him a few minutes ago' routine. By nightfall, the Germans were forced to admit that their star prisoner had got away and that they had made a huge cock-up of the whole thing. Even the dogs they used to hunt down Paddon had led them in the opposite direction to the one he had taken. It had not been their day.

Antony and Fred must have been swearing under their breath, too. They were soldiers, they had done their duty in postponing their own escape for Paddon and did not regret it, but what disappointment they must have felt. They had been working on their escape for nearly eighteen months now, putting the jigsaw painstakingly together and the Squadron Leader had waltzed into Fort 13, planned his getaway with their help and waltzed out again less than eighteen hours later. What's more, he was successful, making his way via Danzig back to England, where he was awarded a promotion and a Distinguished Service Order in recognition of his ice-cool escape.

To make matters worse, the expected backlash was now felt in Fort 13. There was a tremendous purge; no fewer than thirty German guards were locked up as punishment and several lost their stripes. Security was tightened up all round Stalag XXA and escape was impossible. For at least a while, they would have to bide their time. But this sort of drama happened after every escape attempt. They knew the restrictions would gradually ease off and that life would drift back to normal.

Antony and Fred were both itching to put their plans into action. Fred especially, perhaps, as Peggy had recently been in poor health. Instead of a gradual acceptance of the situation, the misery of separation appeared to be only deepening.

Chapter Six

'If anything happened to you, I just wouldn't want to live anymore,' he wrote, in something like despair. 'Please, please, my darling, look after yourself. You're all I've got.'

Just like Antony, he had become increasingly nostalgic for the places in which he had once been happy. He had now been captive in a foreign country for two and a half years and his yearning for the landscapes of his memory grew ever more acute.

'One of the places I want to take you to most is a little village called Mablethorpe on the east coast. Hilda and I used to go a lot with mother when she was alive. Plenty of sunshine, sands stretching for miles; oh there's such a lot of things we have to do together darling.'

As expected, the fever of increased security after the Paddon affair slowly wore off. The Escape Committee put their heads together and again gave permission for Coulthard and Foster to go ahead.

The day before the arranged date, he wrote one last letter to Peggy.

'With every day that goes by my lovely, I get just a little more hopelessly and madly in love with you. Every beat of my heart is for you.'

In writing those words, he must have been aware that, despite all the careful planning he and Antony had done, many things could still go wrong. Some forgotten detail, some pitfall not anticipated or maybe just some stroke of sheer bad luck. Any one of which might well lead to discovery or even a bullet in the head. And Peggy might be a widow before she had hardly been a wife.

On the other hand, it was her birthday in a few weeks' time and, if they were successful, he could be spending it with her in Barnard Castle, walking along the banks of the Tees as the first leaves fell. It would have been a heady vision, one on which he kept firmly focused every mile of the way right across Germany till he finally saw the silhouette of the Alps rising up ahead of him.

What Fred later called their 'stunt' took place on the morning of 21 August 1942. Lance Corporal Antony Coulthard and Sergeant Fred Foster became Dr Neumann and Dr Benecz, two young Siemens executives on a business trip into Switzerland. And what a stunt it would turn out to be.

PART TWO

THE ESCAPE

Note: In this part of the book, the storyteller becomes Fred Foster himself. It is based on various detailed accounts of the escape attempt he wrote after the war, which were discovered in his old suitcase after his death.

CHAPTER SEVEN

On the morning of 21 August, I woke up in my usual bunk, on the thin horsehair mattress I'd now been lying on for two years, three months and eighteen nights. On so many nights, I'd tried to pretend I was back in my teeny room in Bowbridge Road, in the bed I'd slept in all my life. That had been a simple single bed but, compared to the rock-hard one I now occupied, it was fit for the Sleeping Beauty herself. Proper sheets, thick woolly blankets, a fat quilt that my mother had made herself.

Around me, I could hear the usual morning noises: the grunts, the snores, the words mumbled in sleep, the sudden gasp from somebody who'd taken himself in hand to relieve his loveless life. The usual smells were there, too – the ones you never quite managed to get used to. The bodies packed in around you like chickens in a coop, the stale breath of forty men, the damp that hung in the airless chambers even at the height of summer.

Mind you, it was better than in winter when people were often so cold that they slept in their day clothes and sometimes pissed in them, too, the thought of a nocturnal journey to the freezing latrines too hellish to contemplate. How wonderful to imagine that I'd never have to face another winter in Fort 13, that this might be the very last morning I'd ever open my eyes in this damn place.

Not that I'd slept much. I'd been too excited to do more than toss and turn, going over the plans in my head, worrying over some tiny thing we might have forgotten. I'd dozed now and again, the usual faces moving across my mind: Dad, my sister Hilda, old pals from Newark, lads in the battalion and Jack Esam, who was still never far from my thoughts. All those people who had populated the world I'd once lived in before I became a prisoner in a crumbling old fort in a town and a country that was unknown to me, as strange as the dark side of the moon. And of course I dreamed of Peggy. The face that had helped me through the darkness. The biggest stroke of luck any bloke had ever had in this life. And this very morning, when I got up from this bunk and put my feet on the ground, I would be taking the first steps leading me back to her. Whatever happened, even if it were a complete cock-up, it would be worth the risk. Just for the chance of getting home to Peg.

Last night, just before 'lights out', I'd said goodnight to Tony Coulthard as casually as possible.

'Here we go then,' I'd murmured, between puffs of my cigarette.

'Yes indeed Freddie. Here we go,' he replied.

'Think we'll make it?'

'Absolutely,' he said, with his normal breezy confidence. 'But if not, we'll have a bloody good time trying.'

I tried to have the usual breakfast. I was too tense to eat much, not that there was ever that much to eat. Sam Kydd was sitting opposite. Next to Tony, he'd become one of my best pals in Fort 13, almost like the brother I'd never had. He was such a great spirit; always cheerful in spite of the stuff we had to cope with every day. However down you might be feeling, that pixie face could usually pull you out of it with some blue joke about Hitler's bollocks or Jessie Matthews' knickers. There was bugger all I'd miss about Fort 13, but I knew I'd miss old Sam. But the preparations for the escape had been made on a strictly need-to-know basis and I hadn't told Sam when we'd be attempting it. Now though, as he watched me only picking at a bit of half-stale bread, I knew that he'd cottoned on.

'Not hungry today, Freddie?' he asked quietly. 'You sickening for something?'

'No, I'm fine,' I replied, looking down into my coffee mug.

Chapter Seven

'Up to much today then?'

'Just the usual,' I said, hating the lie.

'Nothing special then?'

'No, nothing special.'

I looked straight into the pixie face. There was a slight smile on his lips. I was wasting my time trying to fool Sam.

'Perhaps I might take a short walk later,' I said. It was all I needed to say.

A Jerry guard shouted across with some order. Sam got to his feet.

'Well, mind how you go,' he whispered, giving me a quick squeeze on the shoulder as he turned away. 'Give my love to Leicester Square.'

It was a beautiful August day with the sun baking down. The sort of day that made you glad to be alive. But how much better it would feel to be alive and free.

The time had come to activate the first steps of our plan. During this period, Tony Coulthard was assigned to a working party that left the fort early each day to march out to the site of their labours. Today though, he needed to get out of that. So first thing that morning, a little way along the road, he told the guards he felt sick and dizzy. It was probably the heat, he said. Effing and blinding, one of the guards fell out and escorted him back to the fort.

My own normal journey to work, from the fort to the *Prisoners' Pie* office in the Stalag HQ, was a distance of no more than five hundred yards. It was from this building, rather than the fort itself, that our escape had to be made, so we somehow had to get Tony inside its walls. Despite the short trip involved, everyone was closely scrutinised by the guards. If there were any extras to the regular fifty or so men, they had to state precisely why they were going. The morning passed normally, though I found it impossible to concentrate on my usual round as editor: the reports of football matches and boxing bouts, a review of the latest production in the 'Little Theatre' (*'Private Alfie Stubbs, in a revealing red dress, was irresistibly attractive as Mavis'*).

At midday, we were marched back to Fort 13 for 'dinner'. Again, I tried my best to eat the usual thin fare we were offered. I had no idea where my next meal might come from. At 12.55pm, we were lined outside again to return to our afternoon's work. The train Tony and I had to catch left Torun station at 2pm. Our schedule was tight, with precious little time for any mistakes. The 'sick' Tony now quietly fell in with the column heading back to Stalag HQ.

As the guards came along to count our numbers, Tony started to blow his nose violently, covering his face with his handkerchief. The other fellows, some of whom guessed what we were up to, milled around him, jostling against each other and making it near impossible for the guards to take an accurate count. It was a stroke of luck that one of the guards that day was universally known as Daft Fritz, a bloke so thick he had trouble counting the fingers on one hand, let alone a column of fifty prisoners. He soon gave up trying.

'*Stimmt!*' he said wearily, meaning that all was correct and off we marched to the Stalag HQ.

We got there without further mishap. Having deposited us safely, Daft Fritz and his mate marched off on patrol. Tony and I darted down the passage that led to the door onto the backyard. We watched the two guards move out of sight then we sprinted out and made our way, with much dodging and double-tracking, across the yard, past the guardroom, the Red Cross parcels store and the dentist's surgery, towards the stables where the grooms were waiting for us with our civilian clothes. Fort 13 was circled by not one but two perimeter wires – an inner and an outer. By leaving the Stalag HQ building, we were now outside the inner wire; a forbidden area where only Germans and strictly vetted POWs were permitted. We could have been shot on sight.

But we made it into the stables. The horses of the German officers snorted and whinnied as we flew in through the doors. They were magnificent animals, all of them coal-black, the coats brushed and buffed till you could damn near see your reflection. The grooms were Scottish lads called Willie and Fergus, who'd both been grooms at racing stables in civilian life. Tiny wee blokes, they'd been perfectly cast as 'Munchkins' in Sam Kydd's production of *The Wizard of Oz*. But their statures didn't reflect their characters. They were two hard-as-granite Glaswegians from the Highland Light Infantry who had been captured at St Valery with the rest of the 51st Highland Division. They basically regarded the English, and certainly the Germans, as a bunch of nancy-boys. Brave as lions, they were just the men Tony and I needed to help us get through the wire.

In effect, Fergus's and Willie's roles in our escape were as a form of 'safe passage' between the inner perimeter wire and the outer one. This was possible because of the happy chance that Fort 13 had two stable blocks; the first beside the inner wire and the second right slap bang beside the outer wire. For obvious reasons, Fergus and Willie were among those prisoners allowed to walk freely across the prohibited ground between the two stables. The Germans were accustomed to their faces and wouldn't challenge them

'What kept you?' asked Willie, as he quickly pulled the sacks containing our civilian clothing from their hiding place under the bales of straw.

The four of us went back outside, Willie and Fergus going ahead, carrying the sacks. My heart was thumping away and my armpits drenched. But to any enemy observer we needed to look like a four-man work detail, so I tried hard to look as casual as possible.

With the grooms still about ten yards in front of us, we headed through a short wooded area, which would eventually bring us out onto a lane leading to the second stable block. There, we would change into our civilian clothing and go out through the wire, at a small section that Fergus and Willie had already cut for us. All we'd have to do was to push gently at it and it would open like a door. But to reach the second stables, we had to pass two obstacles, both of them potentially dangerous.

The first was a small house occupied by a German sergeant major. In the middle of his working day, he wouldn't be at home. But to our horror, the fat sod was sitting there, right in our path, dozing on a deckchair in the sunshine.

'Christ,' I muttered to Tony.

'Keep on going,' he replied.' Cool as cucumbers.'

Willie and Fergus had clearly decided to brass it out anyway and walk right past him. But then the bugger opened his eyes.

'Guten tag, mein Herr,' said Willie.

The Jerry was used to seeing the grooms heading to the stables, but who were the other men walking behind them? He was now watching the four of us with considerable interest.

Seeing this, Willie and Fergus clearly decided it was just too risky to go further. They were brave alright, but they weren't foolhardy. As the Jerry watched, they began a great performance of pulling dead leaves off an old withered tree and stuffing them into the sacks that contained our spotless new clothes. Catching up, Tony and I joined in the play-acting.

It was hard to believe it would fool anyone. No less than four men to strip the dead leaves off one tree? Why not just leave them to drop off in autumn? Ridiculous. However, there was something weird in the Hun mentality, that meant if they saw someone performing any sort of task, creating order out of chaos, then all was well and good. Reassured, the Jerry closed his eyes again and leaned back to enjoy the sun.

But the second obstacle in reaching the stables was still in front of us. This was a small three-storey building where about fifty German soldiers were billeted. In the summer weather, there were often a few of them hanging around outside. The four of us had a muttered confer-ence and decided it could be suicidal to go on. We'd got past the sleepy sergeant major but might not be so lucky with any German soldiers outside their barracks. It was decided to abort the mission. Feeling like two burst balloons, we retraced our steps and made it back into the first stables building. Our misery must have shown on our faces, but the grooms were having none of it.

'We'll go again tomorrow,' said Fergus, as he began picking the dead leaves off the clothes inside the sacks, before shoving them back under the straw. It was less of a statement than an order.

'You're not thinking of chucking in the towel are you?' asked Willie. 'We've taken risks for you and we'll not see that wasted.'

Clockwise from left:

Antony Coulthard during his Oxford years.

Antony in the late 1930s with a friend – or perhaps a sweetheart?

The Coulthards at Summer Eights in Oxford.

Dorothy Coulthard pictured in 1922.

Clockwise from top left:

Peggy Urquhart in 1939.

Sgt. Fred Foster photographed before the escape from Stalag XXA, August 1942.

Oil portrait of Fred Foster, painted in 1942 by a French POW.

Fred pictured with his sister Hilda and father Harry while home on leave, Christmas 1939.

Clockwise from top left:

British prisoners in Stalag XXA (Antony far right).

LCpl. Antony Coulthard before the escape, August 1942.

Prisoners in Stalag XXA. Antony's murderer, Hauptmann Mackensen, is the German officer.

Fred producing the New Prisoners' Pie in Stalag XXA library.

Fred's desk in the New Prisoners' Pie office.

Prisoners at dinner on Christmas Day.

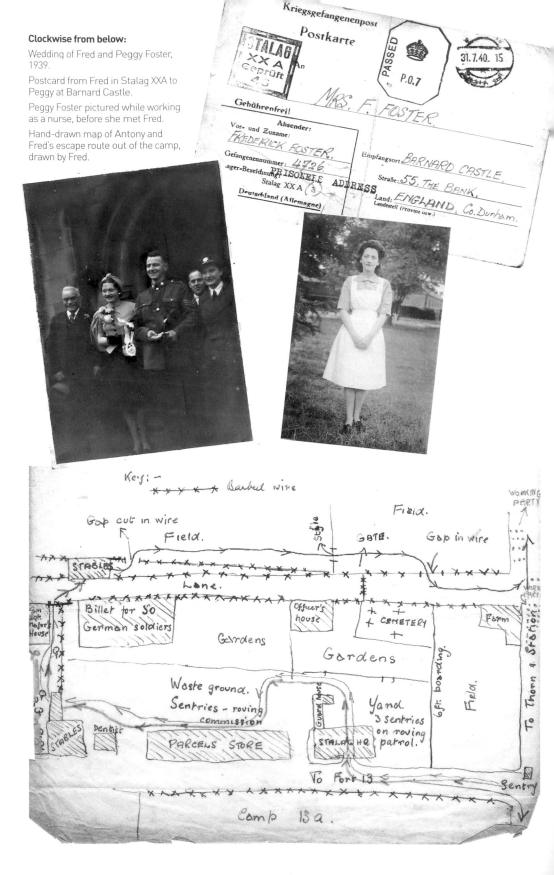

Clockwise from below:

Wedding of Fred and Peggy Foster, 1939.

Postcard from Fred in Stalag XXA to Peggy at Barnard Castle.

Peggy Foster pictured while working as a nurse, before she met Fred.

Hand-drawn map of Antony and Fred's escape route out of the camp, drawn by Fred.

Clockwise from top:
Map of the route through Germany.
The quay at Lindau on Lake Constance.
Unter den Linden, Berlin, in the 1940s.

TEL.
New Milton
894

May 22nd 1945.

VILLA VITA,
NEW MILTON,
HANTS.

Dear Sgt. Foster
I suppose you know
my son Antony Coulthard or "The
Professor' from Stalag XXA perished
on the way home on one of those
rotten marches from Poland.
Cpl. A.G. Price who lives in this
district, & with whom I got in touch
managed to get your address, hence
this letter. I would particularly have
liked to see you, as I believe you
were the Co. escaper with my
son to the Swiss border in 1942, &
from what I have heard, he made
the fatal mistake of returning to
help you at the last moment. Fool
hardy but praiseworthy! And
now he has gone, perished
miserably & unnecessarily!

Clockwise from top left:

Letter from Dorothy Coulthard to Fred Foster,
dated May 22nd 1945, informing him Antony
had died on the Forced March.

Fred finally gets his wish: Peggy and Fred
with Steve and Margaret on a day out in
Mablethorpe, circa 1950.

Fred and Peggy as Mayor and Mayoress of
Grantham, 1957.

Election leaflet for Grantham borough
council, 1953.

Grantham Municipal Elections

St. Wulfram's Ward

Thursday, May 7th, 1953

Vote for
FRED FOSTER

Clockwise from top left: Christmas 1989: Last photo of Fred Foster, with Peggy and daughter Margaret, centre.
Herr Hermann Apitz in 2012. At the age of 13, he was the first to find Antony's body. The barn in Kaltenhof where Antony died.

Rededication of Antony Coulthard's grave, Becklingen CWGC cemetery, Lower Saxony, Germany, 30 July 2015. **Clockwise from top:** Touching Antony Coulthard's headstone during the blessing: Antony's nieces, Barbara and Natasha; Steve Foster; Colin Fulcher; Colonel Jon Murray ADC, Corps Colonel, Intelligence Corps; a Lance Corporal of the Intelligence Corps.

Steve Foster reading the 'Epitaph To a Friend' with the Intelligence Corps padre.

The rededicated headstone of Lance Corporal J A R Coulthard, Intelligence Corps, posthumous Mentioned in Despatches.

'Absolutely not,' said Tony.

'We'll be here tomorrow. Same time, 'I added. 'We English are tougher than we look, chum. Remember who actually *won* the Battle of Culloden.'

'Get your arses out of here,' said Fergus, with one of the few smiles I'd ever seen him give.

We left the stables carefully, eyes peeled for Daft Fritz and his mate, and scuttled back into the Stalag HQ. At two o'clock, the very moment when we should have been boarding a train to freedom at Torun station, I was behind my desk at the *Prisoners' Pie*, my pen in my hand and my heart in my boots.

But Tony then had to somehow get himself back into Fort 13, where he was supposed to be lying 'sick'. This time he was caught. Daft Fritz had gone off duty and his replacement was somebody who could count. What was Tony doing in the Stalag HQ? He was assigned to an external working party, wasn't he? With 'The Professor's' usual quick wits, he spun some nonsense about having a hopeless passion for one of the Polish girls in the censor's office.

'I just wanted a glimpse of her, that's all,' he pleaded. 'Just a glimpse. Have you never been in love?'

Who knows why, but it worked. Maybe the guard himself was currently smitten too, and could sympathise with the agony of Cupid's arrow. Tony got away with a severe dressing-down and yet another black mark against his name. It was a bloody miracle he wasn't thrown into the 'cooler' with the rats.

That evening, back as usual in the fort, we were certainly down but flatly refused to be out. Sam Kydd said nothing, asked no questions, but I could see the disappointment he felt for us written on his face.

'Tomorrow then?' asked Tony as we went our separate ways for the night.

'Tomorrow,' I replied. 'Definitely.'

With legs heavy as lead, I climbed onto my bunk that night. I lay there looking up at the same old damp barrel-vaulted ceiling. Damn and blast it.

But the next day, there seemed to be more guards than usual doing the counting of those going to Stalag HQ. It seemed that Tony's escapade had made the Jerries tighten things up. Any further attempt seemed doomed to a similar fate. The following morning, however, 23 August, things seemed a lot more favourable with considerably fewer guards than the day before. And hooray, Daft Fritz was back on duty.

'Right,' said Tony. 'Nothing stops us today.'

'Agreed,' I replied. 'Absolutely nothing.'

It was another scorching day. Tony repeated his star performance as the man with the worst summer cold in Poland and, with lots more jostling and sneezing, he somehow made it once again into the Stalag HQ.

Strangely enough, the disappointments and delays hadn't made us more nervous or hesitant about executing our plan. They only seemed to have made us bolder, a bit reckless even. Again, we made it safely across the backyard and into the first stable block.

'What kept you *this* time?' asked Willie again.

As two days before, he and Fergus walked in front of us with the two sacks of civilian clothing.

'I don't bloody believe it,' said Tony.

Yet again, our old friend the Jerry sergeant major was sitting outside his house in the sunshine and today his lady wife was beside him. She was as big as he was and the two tubs of lard lay sizzling in the sun, snoring away.

But this time it seemed Willie and Fergus were as determined to succeed as we were. They strolled casually past the two sunbathers, neither of whom even raised an eyelid. Tony and I followed behind and the four of us went out into the lane. As predicted, there were three or four German soldiers at the little barracks, not standing in the lane itself but hanging out of the windows flirting with some Polish girls working in the adjacent field. The presence of the girls was a bit of luck – the perfect distraction from us.

We crossed the lane and went into the second stable block. We dashed up to the loft and made a lightning change. Willie and Fergus had forgotten nothing. They had even brought a clothes brush to remove any remaining bits of straw and dead leaves from the unfortunate encounter of two days before. They stood back to admire their work.

'Dear me, I could fancy you myself,' said Willie.

As we changed our clothes, Fergus had been watching the Jerry soldiers across the lane.

'The bastards aren't moving,' he said. 'They're still flirting with the lassies.'

The only way to freedom was to drop down from the stable loft onto a triangular patch of ground that lay right up against the outer wire. This was where the officers' horses were often left to graze and where Fergus and Willie, under cover of their work, had already made a big enough cut in the wire for us to push through. They'd led the biggest of the stallions right up to the wire and, using it as a shield against any German eyes, had swiftly cut through the fence.

But now we realised there were a couple of Polish girls working in this field, too, picking raspberries from the bushes. They were also the target of the Jerries in the barracks. Crude comments flew across the lane.

'What do we do?' I asked Tony, my confidence wobbling for a moment.

'We have a train to catch Freddie,' replied Tony quietly. 'And we don't have much time.'

It was zero hour. We had to go immediately or we would have to abort our second attempt. Both of us knew, without saying it aloud, that we couldn't let that happen.

'Sure you're clear where the cut in the fence is?' asked Willie. 'To the right of the second bush from the end.'

I searched for the right words to thank them, but of course there weren't any that could do justice to the risks they'd taken for us – or for the punishment they were now bound to face. The fat sergeant major and the soldiers in the barracks had seen the four of us together. Whether our escape was successful or not, the grooms were going to pay a price for it. Fergus and Willie were heading for the cooler and that was that. How could we possibly repay them? But we were British soldiers; this was a war and this was how good comrades behaved. Instead of grateful words, the four of us just shook hands.

'Go,' hissed Willie. 'Go.'

Now I had to jump down from the stable loft. This was the bit I'd been worried about. It was only a height of eight or nine feet but I prayed that the knee I'd twisted so badly a month or two back wouldn't give way again. If that happened, the whole escape was buggered and Tony would be heading for Switzerland on his own. Dropping down from the stable loft, I felt like a parachute jumper landing in German-occupied territory. Thud. I landed right beside the two Polish girls who were startled out of their wits. I picked myself up and dusted myself down. Thank God, the knee seemed okay. I was looking straight into the face of one of the girls. She looked so much like Peggy it took my breath away. The same red hair. The same brown eyes. The same slim figure. She smiled at me. So like the smile that I held in my heart. For a second I was stunned, then I saw it as the best possible omen. This strange thing had happened to remind me why I was risking my life to get out of here and reach home. It filled me with a surge of confidence at the very moment I needed it.

Another thud and down came Tony. He calmly brushed stray pieces of straw and grass and together we ambled towards the spot where the wire had been cut.

What happened next, or rather *didn't* happen, I've never really been able to explain. To say that both of us had a prickly feeling running up and down our spines was an understatement. It wasn't a stray piece of straw, it was pure fear. The Jerries and the girls were staring straight at us as if we were apparitions! I pushed at the wire. It gave way easily. I ducked and was through to the other side, Tony right behind me. Our hearts were thumping like steam engines as we strolled coolly down the lane towards the main road to the station. I prayed harder than I'd ever prayed before. At any second, we were expecting a guttural shout of *'Halt!'* Or even a bullet in the back. Was the view down this lane the last thing I'd ever see? But it didn't happen.

Why not, I'll never know. The German soldiers had seen four POWs go into the stables. Two men in suits had then jumped down again from the first floor. Had they not recognised the same faces? Obviously not. Clearly they had been far more interested in the pretty faces of the women. But even so, when the two men in suits had walked boldly to the wire and exited through a hole, clearly pre-cut, did they not instantly realise that something very fishy indeed was going on? We had remained in their sights for a good minute or two as we walked down the lane, ample time for them to react, stop us in our tracks and investigate who we were. If they had, we'd have been back in Fort 13, banged up in the 'cooler' with Willie and Fergus inside the hour. But they hadn't. Perhaps, stripped of our POW uniforms and resplendent in our new suits and trilby hats, the German mind just no longer saw us as prisoners. Maybe they thought we were Nazi officials investigating the standard of the Third Reich's stabling. Or perhaps they were just spectacularly stupid.

'My God, we did it,' I said to Tony. 'We got through the wire without being stopped.'

'Count no chickens, Freddie.'

He was right. We were simply heading from one spot of bother straight into another. At the end of the lane, at the junction of the main road leading north towards the station, we were alarmed to see a working party marching past under guard. In true Hun fashion, the guards drew back their shoulders as they saw us in our good suits, thinking we must be some big shots. The chaps in the column were all our boys and, despite our civvies, many of them recognised us at once. Of course we knew they wouldn't give the game away, not by even the slightest twitch of a muscle on their faces. Most of them anyway.

'Oh no,' muttered Tony, 'Reg is there.'

Reg was a lovely fellow, but was one of those poor prisoners whose mind had been badly affected by his time in Stalag XXA. His moods veered wildly, going from the depths of despair when he hardly spoke, to periods of the very opposite, when he laughed, sang and chattered away like a demented budgie. The doctors had tried to help, but clearly didn't quite know what the hell to do.

'Pull your hat down over your face,' I told Tony.

But it was too late. Reg had spotted us. A big grin spread over his face. Any second now he'd shout out, demanding to know why we were all dressed up. And that would be that. Of all the little details we might have forgotten, it had never crossed our minds that Reg might be one of them. How vulnerable we were to the tiniest piece of bad luck.

But as Reg opened his mouth, a big hairy hand was clapped over it. Some other hand pinioned his arms behind his back to stop him waving in our direction. Straitjacketed now between his two comrades, Reg marched on past, now harmless as a lamb.

We turned onto the main road a little distance behind the column, slackening our pace in order to let them get well ahead. Suddenly we heard noises behind us. It was a second working party coming our way and we were now sandwiched between the two. Bugger. But that wasn't all.

'Damn it,' said Tony, glancing back. 'It's *my* working party. The one I'm supposed to be on today. The guards all know me by sight.'

There was nothing for us to do but space ourselves evenly between the two columns, between the devil and the deep blue sea, and hope for the best. My heart had started thumping again and the collar of my new shirt was wet with sweat. But we squared our shoulders, never looked back and kept walking. The Good Lord blessed us with another little miracle and none of the guards recognised us.

I now had yet another problem. As part of my new identity as Dr Benecz, the Hungarian businessman, it had been decided I should wear horn-rimmed glasses just like Tony's. But the lenses didn't suit me at all. I could hardly walk in a straight line. I looked like a bloke who'd had a few too many.

'Stop bumping into me,' Tony hissed.

'I can't help it. It's these fucking glasses.'

From the viewpoint of the column coming up behind us we must have looked like a pretty weird pair. But the wisdom of my wearing the specs was proved when a Jerry officer from the Stalag HQ and who knew me well, came towards us on his bike from the other direction. He looked straight at us, but just pedalled on. It seemed our new disguises were working.

Chapter Seven

By now we had reached the suburban parts of Torun, which were situated on the south bank of the Vistula, opposite the old town. This was where the railway station stood and at last we could see it, our gateway to freedom. The working party in front of us now branched off, leaving the road ahead clear. The party marching behind soon fell out also and went off to do some work on the train tracks. Our rear was now clear, too.

But it seemed our pulses were not to be allowed to slow down for long.

'I don't believe it, Freddie,' said Tony. 'Look, another lot.'

Right outside the main entrance to Torun station was yet another gang of our fellow prisoners. They had just arrived back by train from some outlying work site. We got some very strange looks, but again nothing was said. Later on, we'd find out that they'd got back to Stalag XXA, telling people that Coulthard and Foster had 'gone Gummi', which meant we'd gone over to Adolf, as we'd been seen at the station in civvy clothes without a guard. Thankfully, nobody had given us a raspberry.

There was next to no time before our train left at two o'clock. But even those last minutes in Torun were destined to be heart-in-mouth. In the booking hall, we nearly collided with one more familiar figure from the camp, a Jerry guard who knew both of us by sight. Yet again though, this one also sailed passed us with no hint of recognition. In my pocket, my fingers were crossed so tightly my nail had drawn blood.

It was a central plank of our escape plan that, unless it were unavoidable, Tony would always do the talking. If I really had to speak, and people struggled to understand me, he would explain about my Hungarian extraction.

While Tony went to the ticket office, I stood looking at the train timetables posted on the wall. My ears were pricked up, waiting for us to be rumbled at any second. But no, all went perfectly and he came back quietly triumphant with two tickets clutched in his hand.

'Fancy a late summer holiday?' he asked.

The next barrier was a literal one. After handing your tickets to the collector, you had to go through a turnstile to reach the platform. This was where a member of the Gestapo was often posted, double-checking travel passes. But not today. Thank you Lord for another small mercy.

Our train was already at the platform in full steam, doors slamming, ready to move out. We had only just made it. We dived into the nearest carriage. It wasn't the greatest choice. We had leapt into a compartment jam-packed with Jerry soldiers and NCOs who were now staring straight at us. We gave the Hitler salute, had it dutifully returned and sat down. I knew I'd have to make plenty of these bloody salutes before we reached freedom. I could hardly wait to be standing on Swiss soil, finally able to give two fingers to the Third Reich.

I hid myself behind my German newspaper, but not Coulthard. Cocky as you like, he asked the Jerry NCO sitting opposite if he could borrow his magazine. These troops were on leave from the eastern front and soon Tony was chatting away.

'How's it going out there then?' he asked a burly Wehrmacht officer. It was like watching David having a natter with Goliath. But the diminutive Tony had never been intimidated by men bigger than him. His brain was always a match for their brawn.

'We are making excellent progress,' replied the giant.

'That's what I like to hear,' said Tony. 'Damn communists. We must wipe them off the face of the earth.'

'We hope to be in Stalingrad before long,' said the giant, leaning forward confidentially and lowering his voice. 'That should be the turning point. Not long before the swastika is flying over the Kremlin.'

'I envy you,' said Tony. 'How I'd love to be fighting alongside you, but my colleague and I are in a proscribed profession.'

'Don't apologise, my friend,' replied the giant. 'We all serve the Fatherland in our different ways.'

'True,' said Tony. 'Indeed we do.'

I hid behind my newspaper, wishing he'd give it a rest but knowing he was enjoying every second of it. At the same time it came home to me that nobody would have guessed in a million years that he wasn't German. I felt a surge of real confidence that this crazy escape might just work.

Chapter Seven

Gradually, the conversations tailed away and people began to doze off. But I was scared of doing that in case I said something in English in my sleep. I read and re-read the newspaper till the print made my eyes cross.

The train ploughed on across the summer countryside, heading west to our first stop, the Polish town of Poznan. At one station along the route, I almost gave the game away. A frail old lady entered the crowded carriage, looking for a seat. Instinctively I began to rise, but Tony gripped my arm to pull me back down. Apparently, that sort of courtesy no longer prevailed in Hitler's new world. It was a lesson in the need to be constantly careful about my own behaviour. It was exactly the sort of tiny mistake that could have brought everything crashing down around us. Once again, I told myself that I could never have found a better partner than 'The Professor'. My freedom, perhaps even my life, was literally in the hands of this bloke, three years younger than me, so different in many ways, so similar in others.

The carriage was now hot and jammed with people. Everyone who got on barked '*Heil Hitler*' and everyone else was expected to bark it back. I longed to substitute another well-known army word in place of the '*Heil*'.

My throat tightened when a 'Brownshirt', an officer from the notorious SA, climbed aboard. These were the scary boys. The men of the Wehrmacht, the regular German army, were simply conscripts fighting for their country in a war, just as Tony and I had joined up to do our duty for Britain. But the SA were fighting for Adolf and for his ideology. They were the nutcases. No cruelty or dirty deed was beneath them. A young soldier leapt up to give his seat to this one, who took it without so much as a nod of thanks. The old lady I'd wanted to give my own seat to earlier now found herself sitting beside the SA bastard. I saw her pull back from him, as if she was trying to make herself smaller. What a sad, awful place Europe had become. So many decent people permanently cowed and frightened. I kept my eyes down and quietly thanked God I came from a country that was still free. In the presence of the SA, even Tony had shut up.

After two hours, we reached Poznan. Here we had to change trains and buy new tickets for the town of Frankfurt an der Oder.* We'd completed our first stage without incident. Our big bluff seemed to be working so far. But as we walked along the platform towards the ticket barrier, any newfound jauntiness drained away.

'They're the civilian police,' whispered Tony, seeing the uniformed men posted at the barrier. 'Looks like they're checking everyone's identity.'

'Do you think they're looking for *us*?' I replied. 'Maybe the alarm has gone out already.'

Though we were pretty confident about our passes, we couldn't know the answer to that question and decided not to find out. Instead of going through the barrier, we turned tail and retreated back along the platform. When our next train came in, we boarded it without tickets. It was a risk, but not as big as the one that had been waiting at the ticket barrier.

We had a little time to catch our breath but it wasn't to last long. At the very first stop on the route, a little country station, a bloody great horde of Jerry policemen got on. Again, the thought came. Had the alarm now been raised back at Stalag XXA? Was it us these coppers had come for? It just had to be. Yet again, we kept our eyes down and waited for heavy hands to be clapped on our shoulders.

But it quickly became obvious they were merely checking everyone's papers. The territory we were now passing through had once been the original frontier between Germany and Poland, so this was no more than a sort of customs inspection.

'Now we'll find out how well Jimmy Woolcock has done his job,' murmured Tony under his breath, pulling out the *Ausweis* that Jimmy had so painstakingly created.

One of the police came up to us, grunted and held out his hand. Courtesy was in short supply among these chaps. Or maybe they were just bored to death. How could anyone look at hundreds of passes every day in life and not turn into a zombie? The passes were

---

* This town on the Polish-German border is not to be confused with the major German city of Frankfurt am Main.

handed back with another grunt. Good old Jimmy. I'd buy him a pint when we all got home.

The train chugged across the now-redundant border into Germany proper. Bloody hell. The lion's den. Like an actor with a new role, I tried to think myself into the person I was now supposed to be. A young businessman working for Siemens. Until we were safely over the Swiss border, I must try to forget Fred Foster or at least keep him well hidden underneath the well-cut suit of Dr Benecz, the Hungarian with the dodgy spectacles and the terrible German accent.

Tony sat opposite me, gazing out of the window as the countryside sped past on our way westwards.

'Beautiful isn't it?' he said quietly in German.

It was easy for me to guess what he was thinking. On the long evenings back in Fort 13 as he'd tried to drill the language into me, he'd told me enough about his pre-war visits to Germany for me to under-stand how much he had loved it and how distressed he was about the scourge of Nazism and how so many good people had been corrupted by it. It was sad to think about how desperately he now wanted to escape from the land that had meant so much to him.

At the next stop, a middle-aged woman with two daughters came aboard. The woman sat on a small one-person seat on the opposite side of the carriage but, as Tony and I occupied wider seats, the girls came and sat with us, one beside him, the other beside me. The mother had a face like the back of a Newark bus but the girls, in their late teens, were very pretty; though the effect was spoiled a bit by the badges of the Hitler Youth pinned to their summer frocks.

The train rumbled on and twilight came. As a form of blackout, there were no lights in the carriage and we were soon in near-darkness. After a while, I felt a sudden pressure on my leg. I looked down to see that the girl next to me was now lying across the seat and using my thigh as a pillow, presumably on the assumption that her mother couldn't see. What a flirty little *fraulein*. Did she expect me to say something? If so, I didn't want to do that because of my suspicious accent. Did she expect me to steal a kiss? What was I supposed to do?

It was a strange sensation to have a girl so physically close to me again. It was nearly two and a half years now since I'd last held Peggy in my arms. I'll not deny how nice it was to smell the scent of her hair, the softness of her body up against me. I dreaded the possibility of my body producing a natural physical reflex. I was only human after all. For so long, I'd done my best to keep those sort of feelings well suppressed. Most of the POWs who were married or who had a sweetheart back home did the same, finding some release of tension by the age-old method. But plenty of the other chaps didn't, especially those who had worked in the Stalag HQ or in the outlying working parties, in both of which locations there was a fair number of Polish women within easy reach. My old mate Sam Kydd had certainly enjoyed a couple of encounters in his time. Sometimes these were just romantic and never went any further than a swiftly snatched kiss, but it was quite possible to barter stuff from the Red Cross parcels for a brief, fumbled few minutes of paradise. Dear old Sam certainly did.

In any case, this young girl with her pretty head in my lap must have thought I was the most backward fellow she'd ever met. When the dark blue lights of the station at Frankfurt an der Oder slid towards us, I smiled at the girl and picked up my bag, ready to disembark. We had never spoken a single word.

That hour or so in the darkened carriage had been a valuable respite from the stress of our situation but now, spewed out onto another crowded station platform, we were instantly back in dangerous waters. We still hadn't paid for the journey from Poznan to here, so Tony asked directions to wherever we could pay the excess fare. We had no idea what to expect. Would the fact that we hadn't bought our tickets back in Poznan raise suspicions? Would a Gestapo man suddenly appear, take a magnifying glass to our *Ausweises* and rumble Jimmy Woolcock's work in a split second?

But again our luck held and there were no problems. Just a sleepy German clerk who only wanted to shut up shop and get home to the warm embrace of his lady wife. We paid the excess fares and bought two tickets for the next stage of our escape.

Chapter Seven

'*Zwei Karten nach Berlin bitte,*' said Tony coolly, as if we were going on a day trip to Eastbourne.

Berlin. Dear God. We were going to Berlin. We were two British prisoners of war and instead of getting as far away as possible from the Third Reich we were buying tickets to carry us into the very heart of Hitler's capital. We must be crazy. Suddenly, the other routes we might have taken seemed eminently sensible. So what if we'd gone to the east and the Russians had sent us to Siberia? It mightn't have been that bad. But we'd got this far, so the only way was forward now. Besides, I wasn't going to let Tony see that I was having doubts. I also had the distinct impression that 'The Professor' could hardly wait to see Berlin again.

By now it was ten o'clock at night. The first train to Berlin didn't leave until five the next morning. We managed to buy some snacks and a couple of beers from the station café. By God, I thought it was the best beer I'd ever tasted! There was no other choice than to sit it out in the waiting room and try to get some sleep. But there was little chance of peace and quiet. The station was packed with troops and civilians, all of them waiting for the same train as us. It was pandemonium.

But these crowds were a blessing in disguise. We could disappear inside them and stay as insignificant as possible. Had the station been deserted, two men waiting through the night for a train might have stood out like two suspicious sore thumbs.

We needed to take stock, have a private conversation about our progress so far. If we were to speak in English, we had to find a quiet corner and in this place that wasn't easy. You just didn't know who was around you. Maybe there was a deaf person who could lip-read, would realise we were speaking English and alert the nearest Jerry soldier. We had to be careful at every moment.

'I think we're as safe as we can possibly be in this situation,' said Tony.

'They must have missed us by now,' I replied.

'Of course, they have. But they won't have thought of looking here for us. They'll be searching the route to Russia or the roads leading up to Gdansk. That's why this plan is a work of bloody genius, if I say so myself.'

Though we could never really drop our guard, during the short summer night I relaxed enough to ask some German civilian for a light. I felt I really must test myself at least a bit. I just hoped for two things. That they'd think I had a shocking cold. And that they'd never been to the East Midlands. I let a little more of Tony's self-assurance seep into me. I almost began to believe I was Dr Benecz after all.

'If we stood on our chairs right now and shouted that we were actually escaped prisoners of war, they'd all laugh,' I whispered to Tony.

'Maybe, but let's not try it.'

My new confidence was short-lived. Near me was a couple with a young boy, aged about five or six. Being the middle of the night, he ought to have been in bed and was very cross that he wasn't. He whined and moaned and drummed his little fists on his mother's knees. She couldn't make him sit still. Suddenly, I became the object of his attention. He toddled across to me and began to speak very fast. I couldn't understand a word of it. I was totally lost. Tony had gone off to find a lavatory and I was on my own. I tried smiling and patting the kid's head but that wasn't enough for him. He wanted a conversation and I couldn't give him one. Again and again, he repeated the same question and I had no idea what it meant. His mother, poor woman, just smiled at me half-apologetically, but then I began to see that she was finding it odd that I didn't answer the child. I felt a sudden wave of panic and realised that, without Tony right beside me, I was pretty vulnerable. If people spoke German to me slowly and clearly, I would be okay. If they didn't, I was in trouble. Luckily, Tony came back and drew the boy's attention away from me and onto himself. He laughed and joked and played with the child till he quietened down and toddled back to his mother and fell fast asleep. It struck me what a good father Tony was going to make one day.

Despite my own fear of falling asleep in public, I dozed on and off for a while. At four o'clock in the morning, Tony nudged me awake and we moved out onto the platform ready to board the train. There was an immense crowd waiting now. Dead on time it rolled in and there was a mad rush for the doors. We just managed to get ourselves jammed into a corridor. There was no hope whatever of a seat. This stage of our escape, though fairly short, was going to be an uncomfortable one.

It turned out that this was a train full of soldiers on leave from Warsaw. Tony and I had got slightly separated and I was crushed flat against a German captain. I half-smiled my apologies. He cautiously looked me up and down.

'I like your suit,' he said.

'Thanks very much.'

'Lovely fabric,' he said. 'And an excellent cut.'

'Thanks very much.'

I somehow felt I had to say something pleasant in return, though my instincts told me to keep my mouth shut in case my accent aroused suspicion.

'Your uniform looks nice, too,' I ventured.

'I can't stand it,' he replied. 'So ageing. I yearn to be back in civilian clothes.'

His curt manner caught me off guard, and I began to wonder whether he'd smelt a rat.

'Where are you travelling to?' he asked.

'Just to Berlin, then changing trains for Munich,' I replied.

'Love your accent by the way. Where are you from?'

'Hungary,' I replied sheepishly.

He raised his eyebrows. 'Never been to Hungary,' he replied. 'Sounds like a nice place though.'

As the sun came up, the people in the corridor began to sort themselves out a bit. The crush became a bit more bearable and, eager to avoid further questioning, I managed to put a few more inches of clear air between me and my new friend. Further along the corridor, I could see that Tony had managed to sit down on top of somebody's suitcase and dozed off.

Mercifully, this part of the journey was brief, only fifty miles or so. In a couple of hot, sweaty hours, the train was rolling past the suburbs of Berlin towards the city centre and the station for trains coming from the east.

As the train began to slow down, a Jerry sergeant major came out of one of the compartments. He turned out to be the owner of the suitcase on which Tony had been sitting. He grabbed Tony by the scruff of the neck and dragged him off it.

'Get up off there, you bloody fool!'

Heads turned from every direction. There was now a great dent in the top of the suitcase. Frantically, the Jerry opened it up. Inside was the worst sticky mess you ever saw.

'Oh dear, oh good heavens,' said Tony, aghast. 'I'm most terribly sorry sir.'

His stuttered apology wasn't enough. All hell broke loose. The sergeant major began shouting at the top of his voice as only a Jerry can, not just to Tony but to anyone else squashed into the corridor who was willing to listen.

'I am on leave from the eastern front!' he yelled. 'I called in at Warsaw and got some eggs and butter on the black market. They are for my poor Frau who hasn't seen any for years.'

There were murmurs of sympathy from the corridor.

'I am forced to leave it in the corridor in this suitcase and now this… this arsehole… comes along and sits on it,' he ranted on. 'All the eggs are smashed and the butter ruined. And why the hell aren't you in uniform? Something should be done about people like you. By the time I've finished with you you'll wish you *were* in uniform!'

The patriots in the corridor were nodding in agreement, their sympathies entirely with the brave soldier who had suffered this terrible insult at the hands of a non-combatant, a coward in a posh suit. I didn't know what to do. Try to help Tony in some way or stay well out of it. Long ago, back in Fort 13, we had made a firm pledge to one another that if one of us got into trouble along the escape route, the other would try to continue without him. In the event of course, that was easier said than done.

By this point, the train had actually come to a stop at the platform of the Slesischer Bahnhof. We had arrived in Berlin. What should have been a small, quiet moment of triumph had turned into chaos.

Chapter Seven

I signalled to Tony that we should get off the train fast. I said a swift goodbye to the German captain, who seemed sad to see me go. Somehow we pushed and elbowed our way out onto the platform. Instead of our arrival in Berlin being completely unnoticed, we were now the focus of a baying hostile crowd, whose shouts followed us from the train as we walked along the platform with as much dignity as we could muster.

'Fucking idiots!'

'Get yourself into uniform, you useless bastards.'

'You're a disgrace to the Fatherland.'

Suddenly, a half-broken egg whizzed past my ear, quickly followed by a few more. The ruined contents of the sergeant major's suitcase had found a use after all. It was yet another warm sunny morning. Perhaps the platform would soon be dotted with omelettes.

But our luck held. Neither the sergeant major nor his sympathisers were getting out at this station. If they had been, God knows what would have happened to us. If they'd discovered we were escaped prisoners, I'm sure we'd have been strung up from the nearest lamppost and not even the German captain could have saved me.

In the huge station foyer, we stopped to look at the railway timetables. We hadn't managed to discover in advance exactly how we continued our journey from here. The information came up on a big revolving board, but it was impossible to understand even for 'The Professor', so he went off to find a porter for help.

Then something strange happened. As I stood alone waiting for him to return, I noticed an old woman watching me. I looked away for a moment, then glanced back. She was still watching. She looked like a sweet old dear, round as a dumpling, her hair in a bun; like the sort who ran tea shops in Scarborough. As she came towards me, her wrinkly face broke into a nice smile.

'Hello young man' she said. 'Are you and that other gentlemen travelling together?'

Since Tony was now nowhere to be seen, it was clear she'd been observing us for some time. But what an odd question. What business was it of hers? But she seemed benevolent and I saw no reason not to answer.

'Um, yes. Yes, we are,' I replied.

She said nothing more. Just nodded, smiled again and vanished away into the crowd. A harmless old dear, I thought, maybe a bit soft in the head. I was wrong.

Tony came back with the information we needed and just as we were passing through the main doors out onto the street, we were stopped by a very tall, lean man in civilian clothes. With him was the old woman and she wasn't smiling now. The tall man showed us a metal badge that read *Berlin Kriminal Polizei*. In other words, a Gestapo detective. One of the scary boys. And I was scared alright. I saw even Tony gulp. However, this one was at least polite.

'I beg your pardon gentlemen,' he said, 'but one of our lady detectives here has reported to me that you are acting in a suspicious manner. I'm afraid I must ask to see your identity cards.'

Christ, in Adolf's brave new world, even the grannies were spies. We handed over Jimmy Woolcock's little masterpieces of forgery. We'd always worried that sooner or later, some high-ranking Jerry would see right through them. This moment, we were now quite sure, was the end of the escape. Oh well, we'd had a good run.

But we'd maligned poor Jimmy too soon. The tall man studied each of the passes carefully, comparing them with each other, checking the photographs against our carefully blank faces. It can only have been a minute or less, but it felt like forever. I could feel the sweat breaking out on my brow, but I stopped myself wiping it away. That old prickly feeling down the spine was back again. Then, wonder of wonders, the tall man handed back the passes.

'I'm terribly sorry you have been troubled gentlemen but you will appreciate we must do these things,' he said. 'May I direct you to your destinations?'

At this juncture, the sensible thing would have been to gracefully accept his apology and get as far away from him and his granny as possible. But 'The Professor' was having none of that. He drew himself up to his full height, which was about a foot less than that of the Gestapo policeman.

'No you may *not* direct us,' he said. 'And it is a perfect scandal that two businessmen going about the important business of the Reich should be accosted in this manner.'

The tall man looked very uncomfortable, gave the Hitler salute, which we returned, and the two of them disappeared back into the crowd. We moved away from the station area as fast as we could, though hopefully without attracting the attention of any other pensioners who might be detectives as well.

'What were we doing that was suspicious, d'you think?' I said.

'No idea,' Tony replied.

'Me neither. I wish I knew.'

'So do I.'

So what was it? I'd just been standing looking at the train timetables. Tony had gone to the ticket office. What was it that the Gestapo granny had sniffed out? Was it just because we were young men not in uniform? Was it my still unsteady walk due to the faulty spectacles? Or was it something much less concrete? Something about confidence, something to do with the way you carried yourself? Tony had it, that something, bred in a good school and in the quadrangles of Oxford. So maybe it was me, my fault. The bricklayer's boy from 32 Bowbridge Road who'd left school at fourteen. Maybe, despite my best efforts and ten whole years in the solicitor's office, I was still not quite as polished as I liked to imagine. Standing in the station hall in my smart new suit, I had looked somehow out of place and the old woman had sensed it.

I decided that my performance needed to be worked on. Dr Benecz was a businessman, working for one of Germany's most prestigious companies, free to travel across Europe. A young man doing well for himself, even in time of war. Surely, such a chap would appear relaxed and self-assured. Sam Kydd always said that a good acting performance came not from the costumes or the make-up, but from inside. It wasn't enough to look the part, you had to 'think' the part as well. Maybe that was what I had to do. And urgently.

It would need to be quite a performance. As Tony and I walked away from the Slesischer Bahnhof and into the heart of Hitler's capital city, my stomach was tight as a drum. We strolled down Unter den Linden, the wide boulevard lined with lime trees that cuts through the centre of Berlin. All around us were German soldiers with swastika armbands and knee-high leather boots. The great mass of The Brandenburg Gate loomed in front of us, draped with Nazi banners billowing in the wind like the sails of a ship.

Bloody hell Fred, I asked myself, what are you *doing* here?

CHAPTER EIGHT

saw the slap land hard on Tony's face. Ouch. I almost felt it myself. I'd been watching from a safe distance as he approached the woman on Unter den Linden. She was young and very pretty. Blonde wavy hair, bright red lipstick, a pink summer dress that wafted in the breeze against a very nice pair of legs. We'd been eyeing her up for a good ten minutes before Tony made his move. She had been strolling up and down the same stretch of pavement for ages. To and fro, very slowly, looking all around her. She *had* to be one.

But she wasn't. I could just about hear the furious words she was shouting at Tony.

'How dare you sir! I am a respectable married woman. My husband is inside that barber's shop having his hair cut. He will return any minute now and God help you when he does!'

Tony, face as red as a letterbox, was stammering out an apology. It was maybe the only time I'd ever seen 'The Professor' seriously flustered and struggling to find the appropriate words. Bowing and scraping, he walked backwards away from her for a good few yards, before turning and scuttling towards me.

'Let's get out of here quick. Before the husband comes back,' he hissed. 'Come on, let's move.'

We hurried a few hundred yards along the street and dived into a café where we sat near the window but partly shielded by a large potted aspidistra, which we could hide behind in case the lady's husband came hunting for us.

'Sorry Freddie,' said Tony when he'd got his breath back. 'I was sure she was one. I suppose it was the scarlet lipstick. If either of my sisters used anything like that, my mother would show them the door.'

He peeped out from behind the aspidistra at another young woman walking slowly along Unter den Linden. This one wore a tight black sheath skirt and frilly white blouse that did nothing to conceal a chest resembling two barrage balloons.

'What about *her* then?' asked Tony.

'Well she certainly looks like they're supposed to look,' I replied.

'But what *is* that exactly? I don't think we've got any tarts in my hometown. Didn't you have any in Newark?'

'Only the one. Old Nelly. But she was nearly drawing her pension, so I'm not sure she's typical.'

'Well it's your turn now. I'm not making another dreadful mistake. Why don't you go out and ask that one?'

'I'm not asking her.'

'Well I'm not bloody asking her either.'

This was the part of our escape plan that I'd already decided Peggy never needed to know about.

Back in Fort 13, the Escape Committee had strongly suggested that, on reaching Berlin, the first thing we should do was to find ourselves a prostitute. Not, however, for the obvious reasons.

MI9, the section of British Intelligence that existed to encourage and support escapes by POWs from the Nazi camps, regularly smuggled in titbits of information that might help soldiers on the run. One of the latest of these was that Berlin's 'ladies of the night' were often a valuable conduit to the underground resistance. If we could get a girl to take us back to her place, she might well be able to put us in touch with a valuable source of assistance for our onward journey. The long route we'd chosen, all the way across Germany, made us far more vulnerable than if we'd chosen the much shorter, well-worn route north to the Baltic. Any help we could get from the resistance, even if it were just some snippets of useful local information, might smooth our path forward.

I couldn't quite grasp the reason why the tarts of Berlin should be so antagonistic to the Nazis. Could we really be a hundred percent sure that the girl we chose wouldn't betray us to the nearest Gestapo policeman? Unless, of course, Nazi party members always demanded lower rates, so it was purely a matter of business. But the Escape Committee had assured us that this strategy had been used by previous escapees and very successfully, too.

In the end though, it was academic. Though we plodded along Unter den Linden and Wilhelmstrasse for over an hour, we weren't accosted once. Maybe the ladies in question were having the day off. Perhaps it was the celebration of the patron saint of prostitutes. Or perhaps they just didn't fancy us. In any event, we gave up. Since we'd arrived in Hitler's capital three hours before, we'd already been pelted with eggs and nearly been chased by an irate husband. It was probably time to be a bit more discreet.

By now it was almost lunchtime and we were hungry again. Naturally, 'The Professor' knew his way around town and now led me to one of the best hotels. It was like a palace inside. Huge chandeliers, marble columns, deep carpets, a sweeping staircase curving up towards a stained-glass dome. I'd never been anywhere quite so grand. It certainly outshone anything Newark could offer. Tony, of course, wasn't remotely intimidated but it made me feel like a right country cousin.

Using our travellers' ration cards, we had a splendid meal on a veranda in the late summer sun, overlooking the bustle of the street. The tables all around us were filled with Jerry officers and expensively dressed women. The proud Prussian elite would have been appalled to know they were dining in the company of a sergeant and a lance corporal.

It was impossible to believe it was only twenty-four hours since we had sneaked out of the Stalag HQ, jumped from the window of the stable loft and gone through the wire. We hadn't reached freedom yet of course, but we allowed ourselves a brief taste of what you might call 'normality'.

It was the best meal I'd had in almost three years. My last real slap-up feed had been cooked by Peggy's mum in Barnard Castle on the day I'd left for Scotland and the battalion had been deployed to Norway. It was roast beef, Yorkshire pudding, roast potatoes, and jam roly-poly with ice cream. The works. How often I'd thought of that meal in my early months in Fort 13, before the Red Cross parcels started coming and I had to eat the slop doled out by the camp cooks. Whenever I pictured that tender beef and the roasties, the juices in my mouth would start to flow. In the end, I had to force myself to stop thinking about it. It really was enough to make you weep.

Now though, here we were in this grand hotel on Unter den Linden. Despite rationing, the wealthy still seemed able to enjoy the good life. The food was delicious. How amazing to sit at a table covered with a starched cloth of fine white linen instead of our stained wooden trestle table in the camp. I could hardly believe I was eating off fine porcelain instead of a tin plate and drinking a really good beer rather than the piss-poor brew we were sometimes allowed in Fort 13. The veranda was dotted with big marble urns crammed with roses, the scent of which mingled with the perfumes of the glamorous women and the fat cigars of the men. It might have been the heart of Hitler's wicked empire but, after what we were used to, it seemed like a glimpse of paradise.

Going to the lavatory was almost as much of a thrill. After Fort 13's stinking latrines, it was a breathtaking sight. There was a long row of marble washbasins with shining brass taps. Opposite stood a row of individual cubicles of polished mahogany, shiny as the flanks of a stallion. The loo seat, mahogany too, was such a joy to rest your bum on it that it almost seemed wrong to do your business. Perhaps the most wonderful thing was the privacy. I was alone except for an elderly attendant sitting in his own little curtained cubicle at the far end. How nice it was to move your bowels in splendid isolation, without the sounds and scents of Sam Kydd or Jimmy Woolcock doing the same just a couple of feet away from you. At each marble basin there were small bars of soap, each cut into the shape of a swan, and a neat pile of fluffy white hand towels. On a central table was a selection of hairbrushes, backed in mother-of-pearl, and a display of gentlemen's perfumes. I helped myself to a nice big splash of eau de cologne. The old attendant shuffled forward with a clothes brush.

'What a fine suit, if I may say so sir,' he said wistfully. 'I don't often have the honour of brushing down such good quality cloth these days. Not with everyone in uniform now.'

'Have you worked here long?' I asked. The old man spoke very slowly and I could understand him pretty well.

'Forty years sir,' he replied. 'The hand brushing you now once brushed our late Kaiser Wilhelm himself, may he rest in peace.'

Naturally I wished Kaiser Bill very little peace. Eternal hellfire was what that old bastard deserved. The man who'd dragged Europe into war in 1914 and triggered the biggest slaughter in human history. But that was Fred Foster talking and not Dr Benecz, so I just smiled and thanked him and put a coin in his hand. He looked at it with slight disappointment.

'Goodbye sir,' he said. 'Do take care of that beautiful suit. Mind you don't stain the fabric when you're shaking the drops off.'

I found Tony in the lobby of the hotel, talking to a Nazi officer and his lady. God, he knew no fear. Seeing me, he gave them the Hitler salute and came back across.

'What on earth were you talking to *them* about?' I asked.

'Nietzsche,' he replied and said no more. Bloody hell.

After lunch, we wandered around trying to look like a couple of tourists. The Reichstag. The Chancellery. The Tiergarten. The SS and Gestapo headquarters. The Royal Palace, unoccupied now that the present ruler of Germany was a former house painter. Even mad Adolf hadn't been mad enough to move in there.

Berlin was a majestic city and it was a thrill to see it. I didn't like the thought of one of our bombs landing on these splendid buildings, but it was from inside these very places that the orders had gone out to pulverise London, Bristol and Coventry, leaving many thousands dead. We were at war with Germany and much as I disliked the thought of a bomb destroying the grand hotel we'd just left, perhaps killing that nice old lavatory attendant, the soldier in me was disappointed by the few signs of damage in Adolf's lair.

'As soon as we get home, we need to have a word with the RAF,' I said. 'There's too much of this town still standing.'

But there was a purpose to our sightseeing. Whatever we could remember about the German capital might be of some small value to the Allies if our escape was successful. Since our journey had begun thirty-six hours before, Tony and I had been memorising anything we'd seen that might in some way assist the war effort. If and when we reached home, the least we could do was to return with a few presents in the shape of useful information.

The things we glimpsed, not just in the capital, but from the windows of our trains or in the station waiting rooms could well be helpful. Details of troop movements. The position of barrage balloons. Anti-aircraft gun emplacements. But we couldn't just rely on our memories; this stuff needed to be written down. To start making shorthand notes sitting at a pavement café might look suspicious. After our experience with the Gestapo granny at the railway station, we couldn't trust anyone to be what they seemed. Whose eyes were being drawn to two young men not in uniform? That nursemaid pushing a baby in a pram? The ragged man sweeping the street? Even that nun over there? Was there a revolver hidden under her habit?

If we were caught and searched and these papers found, we might well be shot on the spot. Tony led me to a nearby park where, in a far-off corner under a tree, we pooled our recollections of the things we'd noted since we'd left Torun. I took everything down in shorthand and secreted the papers inside my jacket lining. It was a dangerous game alright, but we felt we had to do it. We were British soldiers after all. Tony was a member of the Intelligence Corps. It was our patriotic duty.

'Think of every small scrap of information as another teeny nail in Adolf's coffin,' said Tony. 'We'll bury the bastard one day.'

Sadly, that would never happen. It would be nearly three more years before the world would know the full horror of Hitler's crimes against the human race. Six million dead in the concentration camps alone. By which time the bastard would have taken his own life and escaped the punishment that was coming his way.

But although our 'big bluff' was still holding, every moment spent in this city, every moment spent anywhere in Germany, was a moment too long. We needed to move on and fast. We headed to the Potsdamer Bahnhof, the station from which we'd take the train towards Switzerland. There, another hurdle rose up in our path. Unless they'd been booked well in advance, we couldn't buy tickets right through to the Swiss border. Since Fort 13 hadn't offered the facilities of the usual travel agency, this was one of those small things it had been impossible to find out in advance. Damn it. So we'd have to be content with doing it in stages. Our time in the Third Reich was going to be longer than we'd hoped, but at least we'd made it safely out of Berlin.

As the train snaked its way out of the city, I looked back at the domes and towers of Berlin. It would be a while yet before I got my wish and they came crashing down around the Nazis' heads. But when the Allied air forces made up for lost time and finally targeted Hitler's capital, it would become one of the most bombed cities in history. Russian tanks would lumber along Unter den Linden, past the ruined buildings, and the Nazi banners would be torn down from the Brandenburg Gate and trampled under the boots of Russian soldiers. If the grand hotel where Tony and I had pampered ourselves that day had survived the fall of the city, the old lavatory attendant would be using his clothes brush on the shoulders of Soviet generals. In the future, his face would sometimes cross my mind, as did the Gestapo granny and the outraged young housewife we'd mistaken for a tart. What had happened to them all? Had RAF planes blown them to smithereens? Or had they somehow got through this dreadful war and lived to tell their tales, alive but never quite the same again? Of course I'd never know.

'Well well,' said Tony, studying the tickets. 'Guess where our first stop will be. It's Magdeburg. Gosh. Terrific. It'll be like old times.'

As the train steamed on, he pressed his head against the window, watching for the first glimpse of the old university city where he'd spent the summer of 1937.

'There she is. Look Freddie,' he said eventually. 'Just look at that.'

The twin towers of Magdeburg Cathedral rose up above the River Elbe. Not for the first time, I could see the sad look in Tony's eyes as he came face to face with the beauty of the Germany he'd known before the war. Magdeburg, though far smaller than Berlin, had some of its grandeur. As well as the vast Gothic cathedral, it had fine squares filled with statues and posh, elegant streets of baroque buildings. Despite the war, it still managed to ooze prosperity.

We had two hours to kill here before our next connection and 'The Professor' had no intention of sitting in the waiting room. That would have been the sensible thing to do: dozing behind German newspapers with our trilbies pulled down over our faces. But Tony wanted a stroll down memory lane. We were to be tourists yet again and this time it'd be an even more risky business. Just quite how risky soon came home to me.

'Lunch?' he said. 'I reckon we've got just enough ration coupons left to go somewhere decent. Come on, I know a place.'

He led me across the market square and down a side street. In contrast to the splendours of the hotel in Berlin, it was a nice, unpretentious little restaurant, filled with ordinary folk. Much more my style. We bagged a table by the window and I let myself relax. The feeling was short-lived.

'It's not changed at all,' said Tony.

'You've been here before?' I replied.

'Oh yes, I came here all the time in '37. Charming, isn't it?'

'It wouldn't be bloody charming if somebody recognised you,' I hissed at him.

'It's five years ago. Nobody will remember me now Freddie,' he said. 'Though actually, that waiter over there…'

He indicated a scrawny, middle-aged man serving another table.

'Yes?'

'He always used to serve me' he said. 'I seem to recall he has a limp. Shrapnel in the Great War. But he'll not recognise me now, never fear.'

'But you recognised *him*, so why not the other way round?' I replied. 'Christ, why did we come in here Tony?'

Chapter Eight

The waiter limped towards our table. He was a sad-looking man, as if his spirit had somehow been broken. My heart was racing. Tony, cool as you like, ordered for both of us. Sure enough, the man showed no sign of knowing him. Maybe it was the smart suit and the trilby that made the difference. A far cry from the scruffy student from Oxford who'd cared next to nothing about how he looked.

Tony tucked into his lunch without a care in the world. But mine was sticking in my throat with worry about the limping waiter. I kept my eyes on the big open hatch between the restaurant and the kitchens. The waiter was on the phone. As he spoke into the receiver, he was looking straight at us.

'He's on the phone,' I whispered to Tony. 'He's remembered you. He remembers you're English.'

'I never spoke a word of English to him in my life,' he replied. 'Always German. He serves hundreds of people a year, maybe thousands. He simply will not recall that I was an English student. Relax. Let's have some pudding.'

The waiter brought us some dumplings. They were delicious but I could hardly swallow them. My eyes went back and forth between the street outside and the hatch into the kitchen. Any second now, I expected a black Gestapo car to come screeching to a halt outside and half a dozen scary boys to pour out of it and into the restaurant. The dumplings would be left steaming on the plate as our arms were tied behind our backs and we were frogmarched out into the street and bundled into the back of the car. In the kitchen, the phone started ringing. Again, the limping waiter seemed to focus on our table as he talked.

'Come on Tony,' I urged him. 'Let's pay up and get out of here.'

'Freddie, you really are being a bit of an old woman,' he replied. 'We are Dr Neumann and Dr Benecz of Siemens. Everything's fine. And I want my coffee.'

The waiter brought the coffee and the bill. In the kitchen, the phone rang yet again. Outside in the street a few car doors suddenly slammed. My coffee cup froze in mid-air between the table and my mouth.

119

The waiter came back to collect our ration coupons. He stifled a yawn with one hand.

'Oh, please excuse me, gentlemen. I'm rushed off my feet today. And that phone never stops. Reservations. Reservations. Such is the price of a good reputation.'

I was so relieved I pressed a few coins into his hand.

'Thank you sir,' he said, then turned to Tony. 'Nice to see *you* again too, sir. You used to be quite a regular, did you not? Haven't seen you here for a good while. I never forget a face, you know. Though I wasn't sure at first. You seem to have lost a good deal of weight, sir.'

'Yes, indeed. I've been away for a while. Travelling a lot. It must be a year or so.'

'Oh no, sir,' replied the waiter. 'I think it's much longer than that. Perhaps before the war even.'

'Surely not,' said Tony.

'Oh yes, sir. Before the war. I am sure of it. I am never mistaken in these things.'

'Well, thank you for an excellent meal.'

'My pleasure, sir.'

The waiter went ahead of us and opened the restaurant door. He glanced around quickly to make sure he couldn't be heard.

'Come and see us again, gentlemen,' he said quietly. 'Perhaps when this terrible war is over.'

It was said. The limping waiter knew exactly who Tony was. And Tony knew that he knew.

'I think we've just been spectacularly lucky,' I said when we were back out in the market square.

'Hmmm,' said Tony. At least he had the grace to be slightly abashed. 'I presume he's in the underground. Or a communist. Or maybe very religious. That's about the extent of the opposition to the Nazis.'

'Or maybe just a decent human being,' I replied.

The episode had ended happily, but it might very well not have done. A totally avoidable risk. And out in the streets of Magdeburg, we could easily bump into anyone he'd known in the past: the woman he'd lodged with for six weeks, the shopkeepers he'd patronised, even the postman who'd delivered the letters from his mother back home in the Villa Vita. By now, I was convinced of what I'd often sensed. That the dear, lovable 'Professor', rightly respected and admired by everyone in Stalag XXA for his remarkable goodness and intelligence, also had a wild, reckless streak in his nature. A streak that sometimes overcame all that intelligence. Where it came from, I had no idea.

We still had time to kill before our train. We walked along the banks of the Elbe and through the streets of the shopping quarter. The windows of the grand stores, which I guessed had once been crammed with everything money could buy, were now almost empty. Bizarrely, we came across a branch of Woolworth's with its big red and gilt lettering, so reminiscent of home.

'How about a quarter of sherbet lemons?' I said.

But inside it was a big letdown. Instead of sherbet lemons, wine gums or dolly mixtures, there was only row upon row of framed pictures of Hitler, Goering, Goebbels and the rest of the crew. What a strange sickness had come over Germany.

Eventually we came to the university. On a board outside were listed the names of the professors. Tony knew them all. Again my pulse rate quickened. Again we were pointlessly exposing ourselves to discovery. Any of these men could have walked out of the building at that very second and recognised him, just as the waiter had done. But for a moment, though only a moment, we debated changing our plan. Just as MI9 had informed us about prostitutes being a possible link to the underground who might then help in getting us out of Germany, it was conceivable that academics might be willing to perform the same function. Though more likely than the average Jerry to be liberal, 'free-thinking' and therefore anti-Nazi, they might well be too scared to harbour or help us. And as liberals, it was highly likely that many of Tony's old professors were being watched by the Gestapo. My guts told me it was a bad idea.

'Let's stick to the bloody plan,' I said.' We spent long enough working on it. It's got us this far.'

So we re-boarded the train for the next leg of the journey to Leipzig and then on to Munich. I was glad to see the back of Magdeburg but, as Tony watched the towers of the cathedral retreat into the distance, he must have thought of how much water had gone under the bridges of the Elbe in only four years. And it was as well that he couldn't foresee the fate of Magdeburg. Not long before the end of the war, the Allies would damn near flatten the whole city. Miraculously though, like St Paul's in London, the great cathedral would remain standing among the ruins. A symbol of some sort of hope for the future. God knows, whether in Britain or in Germany, those symbols were badly needed.

Yet again, the train was crowded and I was forced to sit in that portion where two carriages are joined together, a sort of concertina affair that moved and shifted under your feet as the train went round bends. It was far from comfortable and this stage of our journey was going to be a long one.

In a corner, a gang of young men and women were playing cards. They were the usual bunch of youngsters; the sort you get anywhere, just like I had been a few years earlier before I'd seen things I'd never imagined I would have to see. But most of them were wearing Hitler Youth badges. I knew quite well that it was pretty much compulsory for young Germans to join and that it didn't necessarily make them Nazis, but the badges still chilled my blood. It was bad enough that the Nazis had corrupted so many of the adult generation, but it was somehow worse to see them poisoning their children as well.

One of the girls caught my eye.

'Would you like to join our game?' she asked.

'Many thanks, but I'm a bit tired. I'm going to try to sleep.'

She looked at me for a moment, her rosy face puzzled, as if trying to place a thought.

'Are you Hungarian?' she said.

'Yes that's right. Well done.'

I felt triumphant, as if I'd just won first prize in a competition. Tony glanced up from his newspaper and flashed a quick smile. All his months of teaching had paid off. I might never make it as a card-carrying Jerry but, by God, I was one hell of a Hungarian.

Night began to come down, our second night out of captivity. It still felt strange and wonderful to be out in the world again, to be flying across fields and rivers, mile after mile without restriction, and to be surrounded by ordinary people, who were neither British prisoners of war nor German guards. It wasn't a comfortable night, but I'd got well used to those during the last two and a half years, so one more didn't matter. Besides, this cramped and bumpy train was taking me closer and closer to Switzerland. By morning we would reach Leipzig and, after that, head south-west to Munich.

When we left the train at Munich, the air smelt different. I told myself it was the smell of the Alps, the smell of freedom. We were in Bavaria now, no more than a hundred miles from Lake Constance, where we would cross the German border into Switzerland. Only a hundred miles from leaving the Third Reich. In the station lobby, we checked the train timetables, this time as quickly and confidently as possible in case there were any more Gestapo grannies deciding we were somehow odd. By now, it came as no surprise that we'd have a few hours to wait.

We followed the same procedure as in Berlin, strolling round like visitors, seeing the sights. I was really struck by the beauty of these old German towns and cities and, in one sense anyway, had begun to appreciate why Tony had fallen in love with the country. Munich was a beautiful place and no mistake. There were splendid buildings, fine churches and pretty gardens along the riverbank. But our appreciation had its limits. As before, we were still committing to memory anything we thought might be of interest to British Intelligence, then finding a quiet corner to write it all down. The wad of paper inside my jacket lining was getting thicker by the day.

'Come on, we've got time for a beer,' said Tony at one point. 'I know a pub.'

As in Berlin and Magdeburg, he led the way and I followed like a little lap dog on a lead. But by now I was a lap dog with its ears pricked up, alert to Tony taking me for walkies somewhere it might be unwise to go.

His 'pub' turned out to be one of the most notorious watering holes in history. The infamous beer cellar that Hitler and the first wave of Nazis had stormed in 1923 in an attempt to trigger a rising against the old Weimar Republic, which had ruled Germany since its humiliating defeat in the Great War. It was certainly a far cry from the cosy pubs I was used to: a vast barn of a place, big enough to hold several thousand drinkers. Much more than just a boozer, it had been somewhere the intelligentsia, politicians and students gathered to debate the issues of the time; a bolthole for many who were fiercely opposed to Hitler's new movement. One dark night, Adolf and his henchmen had occupied the joint, firing bullets into the ceiling, trying desperately to start the revolution against the existing government. But the Weimar police forces soon arrived in large numbers and nipped the uprising in the bud. The *Bierkeller Putsch* had landed Adolf in prison for a while, where we sincerely hoped he would soon end up again, if the Allies didn't succeed in blowing the bastard up first.

But Adolf had had the last laugh and huge pictures of him peered down at us from every wall of the scene of that old humiliation. His little piggy eyes seemed to follow you around the room. The beer cellar was heaving but we found a space at one of the long trestle tables. As usual, we spoke to each other in German, considering it too dangerous to speak English among so many people. A waitress brought us two tall steins of lager and we clinked them together.

'We're nearly there Freddie,' said Tony quietly. 'Just one last push.'

'I'll drink to that,' I said.

Was it really possible that by this time tomorrow, I would be standing on the soil of neutral Switzerland, in the care of the Red Cross and waiting to be repatriated to Britain? I began to feel that it was. The first thing I would do when I was safe, before I washed, ate, took a bath or slept would be to somehow send a telegram to Peggy to tell her I was on my way home. The very thought of it brought a lump to my throat.

It was now time for that last push. We boarded the train from Munich to Switzerland. The views from the window became increasingly spectacular. Towering mountains covered in thick pine forest.

Deep, lush valleys sprinkled with farms and hamlets. This was the land of mad King Ludwig and his fairytale castles. It was the countryside that had inspired Wagner to write his music, so beloved by the Nazis as a representation of their aim of racial purity in the Third Reich.

Gradually, the train wormed its way down through the mountain passes then suddenly broke out of their shadow into a wide-open landscape that seemed to contain only water and light. In front of us stretched the vast blue sheet of Lake Constance. This massive inland sea, which the Jerries called the Bodensee, was German on its eastern shore, briefly Austrian on the south and Swiss on the west. As the train rolled along the German side towards the town of Lindau, we saw the snow-capped peaks of Switzerland on the opposite shore. No place I'd ever seen had looked more beautiful.

Neither Tony nor I seemed able to say anything. We exchanged a discreet, wordless handshake. In just three days, we'd covered nine hundred miles across enemy territory. The plan that had made the Escape Committee raise their eyebrows to heaven had just about come off. Surely nothing could go wrong now.

The station at Lindau was to be our final stop within the Third Reich. Back in Stalag XXA, it had proved impossible to get clear information about this area so, to a large extent, we were now travelling blind. To our surprise, the garrison town of Lindau wasn't on the shores of Lake Constance, but actually on the lake itself, a small island connected to the mainland by two bridges: one a railway bridge, the other for vehicles and pedestrians. Though Lindau was still a few miles inside Germany, it was effectively the final hurdle we had to leap. From here, the train would carry on along the southern shore, cross into the sliver of Nazi-occupied Austria that bordered the lake and where the train wouldn't stop, then right over the frontier into the safety of Switzerland.

At Lindau, we were told that the train would now stand for two whole hours, while it was fully searched and every traveller's papers thoroughly checked. We'd been prepared for a bigger fuss to be made here than anywhere else on our escape route. It was, after all, the emergency exit from Nazism and plenty of people wanted to take it. But we had total confidence in Jimmy Woolcock's work. It had now triumphed on so many occasions; surely it was bound to triumph this one last time.

As we faced this final frontier, we were suddenly presented with an unexpected choice. At that moment, it didn't seem a particularly important choice; one option no more risky than the other. We were told that for these two hours at Lindau, we could either sit tight on the train and have our papers checked on board or we could get off and go through the same procedure on *terra firma*.

I suppose it was the beauty of Lindau that seduced us into taking the second option. We'd now spent three days mostly cooped up in crowded railway carriages and it was another beautiful day. Through the train window, we could see Lake Constance shining in the sun against the backdrop of the mountains. Beyond the railway tracks, the tiny town looked like a picture postcard. On the side of the island overlooking the width of the lake, there was a grand harbour; its entrance guarded on one side by an ornate lighthouse and on the other by the huge sculpture of a lion. Boats scudded across the water. The sharp, clear light was such a contrast to the damp, dank world we had left behind us in Fort 13. Even if we couldn't leave the confines of the station, we could at least get out and enjoy the fresh Alpine air. By now, we were maybe a little bit drunk on our success so far and by the prospect of freedom waiting just over there on the far shore of the lake. After two and a half years as prisoners of war, can you blame us?

We climbed down from the train full of confidence, feeling the warm sun on our faces. This was it. The last leg of the long road from Stalag XXA.

'Here we go, Doctor Benecz,' said Tony.

'After you, Doctor Neumann,' I replied.

It wouldn't be long now till we could shed our fake identities like the skin of a snake and go back to being Sergeant Fred Foster and Lance Corporal Antony Coulthard. I looked forward to that. No more play-acting. No more talking German. Above all, getting rid of these bloody horn-rimmed glasses that made me look like Dr Crippen.

Chapter Eight

Tony walked ahead of me to the place where the papers were being checked. The border policeman took a fair old while looking at his *Ausweis*, longer than anyone ever had before, longer even than the Gestapo policeman at the station in Berlin. As I say, we'd been prepared for this. This chap seemed to be in no hurry whatsoever, no matter how many train passengers he had to process. He was obviously a dutiful servant of the Third Reich.

But yet again, Jimmy Woolcock didn't fail us. I watched as Tony was handed back his papers and waved on through. It was a wonderful moment. Though his feet were still standing on German soil, he would now face no further checks on the train before it crossed into Switzerland. To all intents and purposes, Tony had made it. He was in effect a free man. In a couple of minutes, I would be, too. In no time at all, we'd disembark in Zurich and I'd be sending that telegram to Peggy. Christ, the thought of it.

Later, I'd wrack my brains over what it was that now went so spectacularly wrong. It can't have been my papers; their design was identical to Tony's. Or so I believed. The appearance of these passes must have been as familiar to the border policeman as his own reflection in the mirror. But was there some tiny flaw, some oddity in the print or the colouring that caught his eye? Or was it something to do with the policeman himself? How many hours had he been working, how many more before he clocked off? Had a wife been giving him a hard time? Had a sweetheart just run off with a soldier? Did he have a bunion that was giving him gip or a bad back made worse by being forced to stand in one spot checking all these sodding papers? Behind his professional front, was he in one of those stinking moods we all get now and again, when you're cheesed off with the world and everyone in it? Determined to give everybody else as rotten a time as the one you're having?

Or was it *me*? Something about me that he noticed and that made him look harder at my papers? Some hesitancy in the way I moved forward? The way I met his eye? A muscle that twitched in my jaw? Just like the Gestapo granny in Berlin who smelt that something about me wasn't quite right? I would never know the answer, but the question would always haunt me.

The policeman started firing questions.

'What exactly is your business in Switzerland?'

'I am helping to sell the products of the Fatherland across Europe,' I replied.

'You have just come from Munich, yes? Where were you before that?'

'My colleague and I were in Berlin.'

'And before that?'

I heard myself giving him our itinerary in reverse, though I never went as far back as Torun. Too risky. Luckily, I understood most of what he said, but my accent made him even more suspicious.

'I'm from Hungary,' I said, trying to smile through tightened lips.

Unlike the girl on the train, he didn't look convinced. Again he peered at my papers.

To my horror, I glanced up and saw Tony walking back towards us. I couldn't believe my eyes. He had broken our cardinal rule; that if one of us got into trouble the other would proceed alone. But he had come back for me. What was he fucking doing? I tried to keep my expression neutral, but I doubt I was successful.

'May I ask if anything is wrong?' Tony said politely.

'Are you travelling with this gentleman?' the policeman asked.

'Yes I am. We are marketing executives travelling to Zurich on behalf of Siemens on business for the Fatherland.'

'I wish to see *your* papers once again, sir.'

'With pleasure,' replied Tony.

The policeman studied both passes, his eyes darting from one to the other, for what seemed like forever. Then he put them down and calmly drew out a pistol.

'I now require you to accompany me to the police station,' he said.

Under the alarmed gaze of the rest of the queue, we were pulled out of the line and, with the pistol pointing at our backs, marched the short distance to the police headquarters. There, our *Ausweises* were put under a microscope and instantly declared to be forgeries. Oh well, old Jimmy had done his very best, but it just hadn't been quite good enough. The 'big bluff' was over but our troubles had just begun.

As they marched us from the police station towards the local Gestapo building, our train pulled away without us towards the mountains of Switzerland. There would be no telegram going to Peggy tonight. There would be no freedom. We were prisoners again.

'Why did you turn back, for God's sake?' I hissed to Tony. 'You knew our agreement.'

'I know,' said The Professor. 'I just thought I should, that's all.'

CHAPTER NINE

The Gestapo building loomed up before us. Suddenly Lindau didn't look so pretty any more.

'Where are your shorthand notes Freddie?' said Tony suddenly in an urgent whisper.

Christ, I'd forgotten all about them. Those scraps of paper crammed with intelligence about everything we'd observed on our journey across Germany.

'Inside the lining of my jacket.'

'Get rid of them fast,' he said. 'The moment we get in there they'll start taking us apart. They'll probably stick a torch up our arses. If they find those papers, we're dead.'

'How?' I was panicking now.

'Stop talking!' shouted the policeman behind us with the pistol aimed straight at our backs.

I don't think I've ever thought faster in my life, before or since. And if I'd ever doubted the existence of God, I believed in Him now, because He suddenly gave me an idea.

The moment we were inside the Gestapo building, I delivered a performance that wouldn't have disgraced Laurence Olivier or Charles Laughton. Sam Kydd would've been proud of me. I started moaning gently, holding my lower stomach. The police demanded to know what was wrong. I turned up the volume of the moaning and groaning.

'A lavatory. Please. Now!'

'He's been having tummy trouble for days,' said Tony. 'One minute he's fine, the next he's in agony. We think it was a piece of pork in Berlin.'

'A lavatory please!' I begged, twisting my body into the Hunchback of Notre Dame.

The policeman with the pistol nodded to a guard. I was taken down a corridor, shown a small lavatory and ordered not to lock the door. Before I slammed it behind me, I saw the guard retreating to a few yards away. As I went on groaning the roof off, I fumbled for the papers inside the jacket lining, tore them into tiny fragments and dropped them in the loo. It was an ancient contraption that Bismarck himself might well have sat on. Please God, the paper would all go down when I flushed it. Still moaning, I pulled the chain and prayed. The water in the bowl started to rise and for one awful moment I thought it might flood over the top, scattering the scraps of paper over the floor like wet confetti. Oh no, not that. Please not that. Both our lives were at stake here. How bloody awful to be shot because of a blocked bog. I held my breath. But with a few splutters and a gurgle, the little whirlpool peaked, then retreated and disappeared round the bend. I gave one last long genuine moan of relief.

I went back out into the corridor, trying to look drained and exhausted. The guard who'd been keeping his distance now came up close to me again. I pointed at the lavatory door and grimaced, my hand wafting up and down to indicate that something extremely unpleasant was trapped inside. If he'd been thinking about checking my activities, he now changed his mind. Maybe he'd just had his breakfast. Farcical though it was, the ploy had worked.

We were taken to a small room at the back of the building. It was a cold, clinical place. There were no pictures on the walls, not even one of Adolf's ugly mug. There were no rugs or carpets on the floor, just grubby, chipped tiles. A small barred window looked out onto an internal court-yard, clogged with weeds and nettles. The room was empty except for three straight-backed wooden chairs, two of them placed side by side facing the third chair, which stood a few feet away. The guard ordered us to sit in the chairs then left the room. We heard a bolt being slid home behind him.

'Whatever happens Freddie, we stick to the story,' said Tony. 'If we don't, we're in trouble.'

'I think we're in trouble already, Tony.'

We sat in silence for a few minutes. All we could hear was the cooing of a pigeon on some nearby roof. The peace didn't last long. The door flew open and three Gestapo men appeared. The scary boys. Two young guards and an older man in civilian clothes, clearly their superior. This third bloke was shortish, but aggressive-looking, with a squashed-in face like a pug dog. He reminded me a bit of the Hollywood star Edward G. Robinson, famous for his roles as violent gangsters. It wasn't a good omen.

As Tony had predicted, we were made to strip off and were searched from head to toe, though thankfully our nether regions were left untouched. Edward G. looked at the tear I'd made in the lining of my jacket where I'd been slipping in my shorthand notes.

'Your jacket looks new. Why is there a long tear in the lining?' he asked.

'It was very hot in Berlin. I took it off in the park and hung it on a bramble bush.'

'Then why was the tear so neat? A bramble tear would have been far more jagged,' he replied. 'What were you hiding inside the lining?'

'Nothing' I said. 'This new suit is my pride and joy. I'm pretty cheesed off about that bloody bush.'

And on it went, but we stuck to our stories like glue. We had no idea, we said, why they had judged our *Ausweises* to be false. They had been organised for us by our employers, the Siemens company, one of the Fatherland's most respected organisations. We were simply two young marketing executives on a business trip. Dr Neumann and Dr Benecz. But the only thing that supported this contention was the forged letter each of us possessed, purporting to give us authorisation to visit Siemens offices all over Europe.

'Is this all there is?' asked Edward G. 'Where are your other business papers? Where are the reports and documents you must surely need to do your work?'

'This is merely a fact-finding mission,' said Tony. 'Getting to know people and building commercial relationships. Gaining impressions of market opportunities for the benefit of our company and the Fatherland. It doesn't really require any paperwork.'

'But surely you must need the names and addresses of the people you are going to visit,' he replied. 'Where are these? I see no sign of them. Or are you both geniuses at committing names, addresses and telephone numbers to memory? If so, I am very impressed.'

'No, of course not,' said Tony, attempting some sort of smile. 'All this information will be provided to us by our office in Zurich.'

Edward G. stared at us for what seemed like forever, then got up and looked out of the barred window on to the scruffy courtyard. There was a long silence. We could hear the pigeon cooing again. Then he turned round to face us again.

'Where exactly *is* the Siemens office in Zurich?'

I opened and closed my mouth like a goldfish. Here it was. That tiny detail we'd forgotten. Something nobody had thought of. And now it was crucial.

'It's down near the lake,' I replied.

'But in which street, Dr Benecz?' he demanded. 'Can you tell me that? Or were you just planning to ask any passer-by once you'd got there? No doubt every citizen of Zurich knows the address of this prestigious German company. An old lady perhaps? The man who hires boats out on the lake? You could ask anyone at all, couldn't you?'

He crossed over from the window and sat back down on the chair. The little pug eyes bored into us.

'I repeat my question, gentlemen. What is the exact address of the Siemens office in Zurich?'

'Konigstrasse,' said Tony.

'Konigstrasse?' replied our interrogator. 'You're quite sure of that?'

'Yes,' said Tony.' Though I confess to forgetting the exact number.'

'Konigstrasse?'

'Yes,' said Tony again.

'But isn't Switzerland a republic? Unlike our beloved Germany, it has never been a monarchy. Why would it name any thoroughfare as "the street of the king"?'

Even 'The Professor' was stuck for an answer to that. Edward G. leaned back in his chair and lit a cigarette. For the first time, the pug face crinkled up into a smile.

'Oh gentlemen, shall we just stop this nonsense?' he said. 'I know Zurich like the back of my hand. I worked there before the war. There is no Konigstrasse. Your whole story is as false as your travel papers. I have been amusing myself with you but now I am becoming a little bored. So you will please tell me exactly who you are and why you are trying to leave Germany and enter Switzerland. And you will tell me now.'

It seemed pointless to go on spinning our yarn. He hadn't swallowed a word of it. Surprisingly, the only thing he did swallow, hook, line and sinker, was that Tony was German and I was Hungarian. And it was pretty clear he believed we were engaged in some form of espionage against the Third Reich. As the native Kraut, rather than just a pesky Hungarian, Tony was given a rougher interrogation than I was. How could any child of the Fatherland stoop to betraying it?

In the eyes of the Gestapo, there was no greater sin. It was their patriotic duty to knock us around a bit. It wasn't very pleasant. In fact it was hellish. Presumably the floor was tiled for the easier mopping of blood or the sweeping up of broken teeth. We took the slaps, the kicks and the punches as best we could. Still, Tony and I stuck to our story. We stiffened our upper lips, turned the other cheek and tried to remember we were British soldiers. In my head, I repeated my name, rank and serial number over and over. I knew that this could get a lot worse than a cut lip and a bruised rib.

And gradually it did get worse. Not physically, but in the dawning realisation of what Edward G. and his thugs were planning to do with us. First they stopped knocking us about and, oddly, the heavy silence in the room was more frightening than the punches and the kicks. We were now formally charged with spying against the Third Reich. Then they weighed us. Measured our height. Took our photographs. All of which could only mean one thing. The crime they believed us to be guilty of was infinitely worse than the one we had actually committed: being escaped prisoners of war. I suspected that the door leading out to the scruffy courtyard would be my exit from this world. We were about to be executed.

For some reason, we were briefly left alone in the interrogation room, though with a guard posted outside.

'Tony, the game's up,' I said in English. 'We've got to drop this nonsense and confess our real identities fast.'

'And back to Fort 13?' he said.

'Better back to Fort 13 than not getting off this island alive!' I replied. 'Can't you see they're about to fucking shoot us?'

So we changed our story. We shed the skins of Dr Neumann and Dr Benecz and confessed that we were British POWs escaped from Stalag XXA in Torun, Poland. I'd thought this would immediately save our bacon, but it didn't. It became crystal clear that the Jerries no more believed the truth than they'd believed the lies. Two POWs from Poland couldn't possibly have travelled nearly a thousand miles across The Reich, said Edward G. Nor could we ever have been able to obtain such smart clothing. Above all, the Jerries simply couldn't accept that someone with Tony's fluency in their language could be anything other than a card-carrying Hun. It looked like the chief asset in our escape attempt, the bluff on which everything had been based, had suddenly turned into our greatest danger. Christ, were they going to shoot us anyway?

'Just telephone the Commandant at Stalag XXA,' I pleaded. 'Ask if Sergeant Fred Foster and Lance Corporal Antony Coulthard are escaped prisoners.'

It took a lot of persuasion but finally the call was made. The Commandant, pretty embarrassed of course, admitted to the much-feared Gestapo that he had indeed lost two of his inmates a few days before.

So the show was over. Thank God they'd never found the shorthand notes that, British POWs or not, would almost certainly have led to us being executed in that courtyard. I prayed that the paper would never gurgle back up that U-bend in the Gestapo bog. But at least we'd saved our skins. A while later, we were escorted under guard out of the Gestapo headquarters into the fresh air; something I'd seriously doubted we would ever do again. Around us, the people of Lindau were going about their daily business, the sun was still shining, the boats were out on Lake Constance and the Swiss Alps were still over there on the skyline. But we were heading in the other direction, back to where we'd come from. We had been so near – so bloody near it almost broke my heart.

The Gestapo now washed their hands of us and handed us over to the loving care of their chums the Wehrmacht, the Jerry military. The pistol came out again and we were marched to the old fortress of Lindau and thrown into what wasn't so much a cell as a dungeon. It felt a bit like being flung into the Tower of London. It was hard to believe that such a pretty town could possess such a chamber of horrors and the worst horror was the rats. It was hard to get any sleep with the little furry bastards scurrying around our feet. Where was the Pied Piper of Hamelin when you needed him?

Rats or no rats, I doubt I'd have slept much. That night we should have been in Zurich. We would have already sent telegrams to our families. We should have been having a good dinner somewhere overlooking the lake and drinking a little too much. We should have been free men.

Instead, the chilly gloom of the dungeon was an appropriate setting for how we both felt. We were exhausted, drained by the day. We didn't make much conversation, but there was one question I couldn't help but ask again.

'*Why* did you come back for me Tony? You could have been free.'

The Professor just smiled and didn't reply.

*

Chapter Nine

It was grim to wake up the next morning in that blasted place, our hopes all gone.

The only good thing was that they now moved us out of the fortress and into a nearby military prison, which was a bit more civilised. We were to be kept here until an escort arrived from Stalag XXA to take us back to Poland, which would obviously take a few days. Till then, we were put into one small cell, eventually given a small bowl of soup and allowed to wash, though only under strict guard. Ironically, from the window over the tub where we washed, we could see right across Lake Constance to the shores of Switzerland. At this southernmost point, the lake was only a mile or so wide and we could just about make out Swiss sunbathers on the beaches opposite. Beach huts and bright parasols and tiny figures stretched out on the shore.

No medieval rack or any other device of torture could have been worse than the pain of that view. To any prisoner, the sight of 'normality' really hurts. It is the thing you yearn for above all else and the thing you can never have until you are free. Did all those dads, mums and kids on that opposite shore know how lucky they were? No, of course not. How could they? Lying by the lakeside, splashing in water, taking out a rowing boat – all of that they could take for granted. I remembered writing to Peggy from Fort 13 that one day I would show her the beach at Mablethorpe where my parents had often taken my sister and me as kids. I loved it there and one day I was determined I would sit on that beach again, but this time as a husband and a father, paddling in the shallows with my own children, building them sandcastles and wiping ice-cream off their chins.

Looking out through the barred window of our cell, it was necessary to remind ourselves firmly that we were only behind these bars because an evil had come into our world that threatened all those normal, everyday joys and that we had been forced to stand against it. If such simple freedoms were ever to be lost, God help us all. That was why Tony Coulthard and I, Sam Kydd, Jimmy Woolcock, Willie and Fergus and tens of millions of other men and women had said their painful goodbyes on railway platforms and enlisted in armies, navies and air forces. Reluctantly, we'd learnt how to use weapons that could kill other human beings, something which, after the slaughter of the Great War, we'd never imagined we might have to do. We'd gone off to fight in those far corners of foreign fields. Many of us would die and those who survived would never be quite the same people again. So as I stood there at the tub, doing my best to wash and shave, I didn't hate the comfy Swiss having fun on the opposite side of the lake. I was glad for them but also doubly determined that somehow our escape attempt was not yet doomed and that we would still get out of here. God knows how. And I wished He would tell me quickly.

Our latest prison comprised two long corridors, on the ground and first floors, each flanked with cells. In the door of each cell was a small grille. The doors were locked by two large bolts on the outside, which shot home into the iron doorframe. It turned out that all the other prisoners were members of the German Army who'd got themselves into some disgrace or other, like desertion, absence without leave or just shouting 'Fuck the Führer' after a few lagers too many.

In the light of day our spirits revived a little. Tony and I sat in our cell and debated ways and means of getting out of here and across to that Swiss shore, so temptingly close.

'We could swim it,' I suggested, stating the bleeding obvious.

'Maybe *you* could, but I'm a lousy swimmer,' he replied.

'Well that's no good then.'

'You could try it without me.'

'Go without you?' I asked.

'Yes.'

'I hardly think so, do you?'

Suddenly we heard whispering coming from below the outside window of the cell. A succession of curious German faces were pushed against the bars. It turned out we had become local celebrities and the jailer had brought his cronies to view the two 'genuine Englanders' who had nearly got across the lake to freedom.

'Bugger off!' I shouted and, to my surprise, they did.

As darkness fell, we began to settle down as best we could on the wooden planking that was to be our beds. We were still talking of our chances of getting away before the escort from Poland got here, when a noise like a machine gun burst out in the corridor above.

'What the hell's that?' I said. 'Are they shooting people?'

Maybe the Jerries had decided not to bother with transporting us back to Stalag XXA. Maybe they were just going to kill us after all. A lot quicker. A lot less paperwork and inconvenience and damn the Geneva Convention.

The machine gun noise was repeated several times, always getting closer. Was this it? Was this curtains for Coulthard and Foster? After about ten minutes, we heard footsteps along our corridor, then the huge bolts on our door shot back. A figure entered the cell. He was clothed in a ragged pair of trousers and a filthy vest without boots or socks. He came in on tiptoe, his finger to his mouth.

'Ssssh!' he said, closing the door. 'Sprechen Sie Deutsch?'

Tony asked him what he wanted. He replied that he was an NCO and was banged up in this dump for being late back from leave.

'I heard you were Englishmen,' he said. 'And I wanted to see what you looked like. I have never seen one before.'

He told us that the jailer went home every night at seven, leaving all the prisoners locked up unattended. He had learned how to open his cell door from the inside with the use of a piece of wire. This had been the machine-gun-like noise we'd just heard from above. The noise didn't matter as there was no jailer there to hear it.

A bizarre story unfolded. This chap had a girlfriend in Lindau. Every evening he sneaked out of the prison, saw his girlfriend who gave him a good meal and other sorts of nourishment, and returned in the morning before the jailer arrived. Nobody knew he'd ever been gone. Tony and I were a bit wary of these confessions. It might well have been some trap by the Jerry intelligence, so we just answered by smiling or shaking our heads.

Our new friend was pretty cheesed off with his own side. For being three measly days late back from leave, he'd been given six months' imprisonment and stripped of his rank.

'It is so unfair,' he said. 'I am an important man. The leader of the platoon of assault boats on the lake. I help to train the new recruits. It is vital work for the Fatherland. I should have been treated with a lot more respect, don't you think?'

Tony and I looked at each other. The germ of the same idea formed in our heads at the same moment. But still we were cautious and merely listened, grunting the odd bit of sympathy.

'But I must go now,' he said. 'My girlfriend will be waiting for me.'

He winked and his hands imitated the curves of a particularly voluptuous figure. He'd drop in on us again the next evening, he said. Closing the bolts on our cell door, he went off down the corridor. We heard the outside door of the little prison being opened and shut again. And off he went, like a tomcat, on his nightly prowl.

'Right then Freddie, how do we use this bloke to get us out of here and across the lake?' said Tony at once.

We discussed the scraps of information 'Tom Cat' had given us. In the conversation, he'd shown great curiosity about life in England, repeating one particular question several times.

'How much does a chef in a hotel earn per week?' he'd asked.

It seemed he was interested both in getting out of Adolf's Germany and in a complete change of career.

The next morning we washed again in the tub that looked out over the lake. That Swiss shore really was tantalisingly close. We were given breakfast: a crust of bread and some ersatz coffee. Today, the jailer seemed inclined to talk. For some reason he was fascinated by the suits we were still wearing. Were they English? No, we told him. But they were of such good cloth and cut, he said. No German could possibly get one of such quality. We answered his questions guardedly, in order to protect the Polish underground back in Torun and the tailor who had made them.

'You can have the suits,' I told him. 'In return for some other clothing. Anything will do. We're not fussy.'

This was a dangerous ploy. Why would we want to make such a nonsensical exchange? And this bloke wasn't stupid.

Chapter Nine

'Were the particulars of your clothing written down at the police station?' he asked in a low voice.

No, we said, which was a black lie. The jailer was clearly weighing up the risks to himself if he made the swap. But it was obvious he really wanted those suits. In the deprivations of wartime, things that had once been everyday items could acquire a ridiculous status.

We still had about four hundred marks and some of our travellers' ration cards, so we asked if he could use the coupons to buy us better food than the pigswill on the prison menu. He agreed and came back at midday with half a loaf, some cheese and two bottles of beer. He watched as we ate, then announced that he had something to show us. Going off to his little billet, he returned with a rather worn lounge suit. It was all he could manage to find, he said. Since he was nearer Tony's size than mine, he would take Tony's suit in exchange for his own, if we would promise to say nothing. 'The Professor' agreed and bid a sad goodbye to the perfect piece of tailoring in which he'd so recently strolled down Unter Den Linden.

The long day wore on, then shortly after seven in the evening the bolts on our door slid back again and this time not one but two dilapidated figures came in. Tom Cat had brought a friend to visit. A former member of the assault boat platoon, this man was a butcher by trade, in jail for killing a pig without informing the authorities. Like Tom Cat, this chap was very disgruntled by his treatment at the hands of his own side. As on the evening before, we were quizzed again about England. We proceeded to give them both a very rose-tinted picture of life back home. Tony used all his dramatic talents to lay it on with a trowel. The White Cliffs of Dover. The lights of Piccadilly Circus. The quality of the beer.

'And what about the women?' asked Tom Cat, who was clearly a bit of a Lothario. 'I have heard they are very shy, very cold. You cannot even kiss them unless you have proposed marriage.'

'Nonsense,' I replied. 'British girls will love a big strapping lad like you.'

'And they do not all look like Gracie Fields?' he asked.

141

'Oh no, not at all,' said Tony. 'And being a chef in a London hotel would be a very luxurious life. Pretty girls on tap, twenty four hours a day.'

'How much would a chef earn?'

'At least ten pounds a week plus tips,' replied Tony, who hadn't the foggiest idea.

'And what about a butcher?' Tom Cat's friend piped up.

'Almost as much,' replied Tony, 'plus all the pigs you could possibly want.'

This last answer was an especially black lie. Rationing was now well underway in Britain. Year by year, more and more things had become restricted. These days, most of the British population could only dream of roast pork.

Other questions came thick and fast. What would be the British Government's attitude towards Germans who came over into the British lines?

'Do you remember in The Bible the story of the Prodigal Son?' said Tony. 'When you come to England, it will be like that. There will be feasting and rejoicing that you have seen the light.'

'So if we help you both to escape from here, we would not be interned when we got to Britain?'

'Absolutely not,' I replied. 'And after all, wouldn't there be two fewer Germans fighting in the war?'

Tony and I had discussed the morality of all this the previous evening and decided that such blatant deceptions were justified by what the Jerries had done to us for the past two and a half years. Tom Cat and his chum retired into a corner of the cell and engaged in deep conversation for a good ten minutes. Then came their proposition.

'I still have the key to my assault boat on the lake,' said Tom Cat. 'It's moored about half a mile from here. There are about ten of these boats altogether so there's always a guard kept on them. At night, there's also a searchlight, which plays over them about every ten minutes, so stealing a boat would have to be done fast, but I can do it.'

'What about the lake?' I asked. 'Isn't it mined?'

'Yes and there's barbed wire, too, but I know exactly where the mines and the wire are.'

'You're absolutely sure about that?' said Tony.

'Yes. So, are you in earnest?' asked Tom Cat.

'Definitely,' I replied.

'This is our plan then. Tomorrow night at eleven o'clock, we'll fetch you from your cell and get you out of here. We know a quiet back way that will lead us to the boats.'

'What about the guard?' I asked.

'We'll have to disable him somehow,' said Tom Cat. 'Knock him out or bind and gag him.'

'Okay, but no killing,' said Tony. 'We don't want his blood on our hands.'

'Neither do we,' said Tom Cat.

'And then?'

'After the searchlight has swept over all the boats, we wade out to my particular boat. Once we're on it, we paddle her out for a bit, then I start up the motor. They're always kept filled with petrol.'

'But won't they shoot the moment they hear the motor?' I asked.

'Yes, but the boats are armour-plated. If we lie down inside the hull, we'll come to no harm. These boats go like bats out of hell. Once we get out of their range, nothing can stop us.'

'Then what?'

'They'll probably send up a plane with searchlights to chase us but when we reach the Swiss shore, there's not much they can do. We'll run up the beach and hide in a wood that we know well. At dawn, we walk into the village of St Gallen and give ourselves up to the Swiss authorities. That's our part of the bargain.'

'And ours?' Tony asked.

'You tell the British authorities how much we've helped you, so that they don't intern us in England.'

'It's a deal,' we said.

We were excited. Hope flooded back into our veins after the desolation of our capture forty-eight hours before. But in our conversations with him, there had always been a whiff of suspicion hanging in the air. On both sides. Tom Cat then decided to express his openly.

'If there is any funny business from either of you, I have a knife and I won't hesitate to use it,' he said.

We assured him we had no interest in funny business, which was true. All we wanted was to get to the other side of that lake. Anything else we'd worry about later.

Tom Cat went off on his evening visit to his sweetheart. Presumably, he wouldn't be telling her that tonight was the last time he'd be eating her apple strudel or enjoying the delights of her bed. If she'd ever dreamed of being Mrs Tom Cat, she was going to be disappointed.

I don't know how Tony and I got through that night. Neither of us slept much but just lay silently in the dark, each with his thoughts. Might we really snatch victory from the jaws of defeat? Our escape plan, our 'big bluff', so carefully thought out, had come unstuck. Fifteen months of endless evenings in Fort 13 with Tony drumming German into my thick head had come to nought. All the effort and risk taken by so many others, both our British mates and the Polish underground, had been wasted. We were still sitting in one of Adolf's cells. Albeit one with a much nicer view. But was it now possible that we might succeed in getting to freedom thanks to two German soldiers who were in a bad mood with those above them? I decided that stranger things had happened. Like the good Lord, fortune worked in mysterious ways.

All through the next day, minutes seemed like hours. Tony and I sat in our cell drumming our fingers. We conjured up visions of sending a funny postcard from Switzerland to the Commandant of Stalag XXA. We played noughts and crosses on the wall. And we talked, too, perhaps more intimately than we had ever done before.

He told me about his years at university, painting pictures of a life I wished I'd had. He talked about the joy of study for its own sake rather than, as I'd experienced it as a solicitor's clerk, merely for the sake of 'getting on', putting bread on the table and a roof over your head. I envied him the sort of experiences that few bricklayers' sons could ever hope for. He talked about how hard it had often been to live up to the expectations of his parents, but how grateful he was to them for the sacrifices they had made to let their children make the best of themselves. I wondered if he regarded getting captured at Amiens in 1940 as possibly being some sort of failure in their eyes.

We talked about what might happen to us after the war. We assumed, of course, that the evil of Nazism would eventually be destroyed; any other outcome was quite unthinkable. Old Churchill's blood, sweat and tears would not be for nothing. The fight on the beaches, on the streets and in the hills would be worth it in the end. And when the victory came, things would change in Britain. The worst of the old ways would be swept aside. Life would be fairer for everyone. It would be a society where the kids of army captains and of bricklayers would have the same chances. It would be some sort of brave new world.

I talked to him about Peggy, how we'd met and how incredible it was to suddenly encounter another human being with whom you knew, without the slightest doubt, that you wanted to share every-thing in this life. In sickness and in health, for richer for poorer, and all those other vows that you'd learned like a parrot and made a bit nervously at the altar but that you meant with every fibre of yourself. It was like being hit by a tidal wave, I said, and one day it would happen to him. 'The Professor' laughed and took off his glasses to give them a clean, something he always did when he felt a bit awkward.

First of all though, we needed to get out of this bloody cell. The day dragged on endlessly. It was as if my body was on red alert, ready for whatever was about to happen. My senses seemed sharpened: sight, sound, smell, all felt more intense. Instead of another night in this prison, we will be sleeping under the stars in the wood in Switzerland. We were like two caged creatures, ready to spring the moment the cage was opened. The clock was ticking. The countdown to our second chance of freedom had started.

But at six-thirty on that late summer evening, just four and a half hours before we were due to escape, the clock stopped. As we paced around our cell, we suddenly heard the tramp of booted feet coming along the corridor outside. The bolts on our door were thrown back. The jailer stood framed in the doorway.

'Time to go, gentlemen,' he said.

'What do you mean?' I asked. 'Go? Go where?'

'The arrangements have been changed,' he replied. 'Instead of waiting here for the escort to take you back to Poland, you're to be taken to the camp at Memingen to wait for them there.'

We were stunned but tried to act as if we hardly cared.

'But it's late. Can't we go in the morning?'

'No. The guard has arrived to take you now. Let's go.'

Like zombies, we gathered our few bits and pieces and moved in slow motion out of the cell. The jailer looked at us shiftily. Tony, of course, was now wearing the jailer's old suit. He'd have been a fool not to know we'd been planning an escape and he wasn't a fool.

We were marched straight to the station. The same station we'd arrived at only two days before, so happily inhaling the Alpine air. We were put on a train that crept back across the short bridge from the island of Lindau to the German mainland. The Alps receded behind us into the dusk, almost as if they had only been a figment of our imagination. Two hours later we arrived at Memingen, which was a camp for mostly French prisoners.

That night, instead of sleeping under the trees, we lay in yet another prison cell. Our dreams of getting home had vanished. And poor Tom Cat would never be a chef at the Ritz or sleep with a welcoming English maiden.

As our old chum Sam Kydd would write many years later in his memoir of Stalag XXA, the escape attempt of Coulthard and Foster was 'a glorious, successful, heart-breaking failure'.

I suppose that about sums it up.

CHAPTER TEN

It was nine hundred miles of misery. Our return journey to Stalag XXA was somehow far worse than the one we'd both made two and a half years before. There were no cattle trucks this time, but mentally it was just as bleak.

When he'd collected us at Memingen, our Jerry escort had asked for an undertaking that we wouldn't try to escape again. We'd refused point blank and so we travelled the whole nine hundred miles at the point of his pistol. We recognised his face, but hadn't known him well in the camp. He was a sergeant, known to the prisoners as Happy Heinrich because he rarely smiled. Like most of the guards at Stalag XXA in Torun, he was an older man; pushing fifty maybe, a bit overweight, well past his best for active military service. No doubt he'd volunteered for this job: a nice little break from the essential boredom of a POW camp. A chance to enjoy the scenery, get out from under the eye of his superiors and have a few more beers than normal, at least on his outward journey.

Though we'd refused to promise to be good boys, in truth I'm not sure we had the stamina left to make any fresh attempt at escape. We'd just been through four or five days on a rollercoaster, from the heights of excitement to the depths of despair. We were both so drained that we'd surely have made stupid mistakes. We no longer had any papers, money or travellers' ration cards. If we'd tried anything, the chances are we'd soon have landed back exactly where we now were. With a pistol at our backs. There seemed to be bugger all point.

The route back across Germany was to be different to that of our outward trip. After passing back through Munich, we next reached the town of Augsburg. From there we were supposed to take another train on to Nuremberg, but the train at Augsburg was jam-packed with both German and Italian soldiers. It was so overloaded they were practically hanging out of the windows. Happy Heinrich asked the station master if we could travel in the guard's van.

'These are two desperate characters,' he said. 'I have to get them back behind bars as quickly as possible.'

But the station master refused. The military might run the country, he said, but he ran his own damn station. We would just have to wait for the next train like everyone else. It didn't get there a minute too soon, because just as it began to pull out of Augsburg with the three of us now on board, a heavy Allied air raid began. In no time, it seemed that the whole town was ablaze. We gazed at the conflagration from the window as the train sped away; fires licking around the copper-domed towers of the churches.

'That's one of the oldest cities in Europe,' said Tony sadly. 'Founded by the Romans. It has survived wars for nearly two thousand years. And now look what's happening to it. God, this war.'

But the blunt truth was that it was also a major military base and, more importantly, the place where they built Messerschmitt aircraft. Who could blame our boys for putting it in their sights? Our train might now have been going at full throttle, but so that night was British Bomber Command and Nuremberg was in its sights, too. We were merely fleeing from one danger-zone straight into another.

Next to Berlin itself, no German city had greater significance in the eyes of the Allies. In the 1930s, this was where Hitler had addressed massive rallies of his disciples, tens of thousands of Nazi bastards goose-stepping and saluting like clockwork soldiers. These were the first images of Hitler's Germany that most British folk ever saw – in the Pathé newsreels at the pictures on a Saturday night. How we'd all laughed at them, though we'd stopped laughing pretty quickly.

Just as we reached the outskirts of the city, the sirens sounded, the train ground to a rapid halt and the lights in the carriage went out. Heinrich began to get a bit tense.

'Don't try anything,' he said, 'or I'll shoot you.'

Regardless of the fact that he might well have missed in the blackout, it was unlikely we'd have got very far, even if we'd managed to get off the train. All night long we could hear the dull boom of the bombs in the near distance. In Berlin, I'd said to Tony that the RAF seemed to be slacking when it came to bombing German cities, but now these words came back to haunt me. Like Augsburg, Nuremberg was an important centre for building aircraft, submarines and tanks and, as if they'd overheard me, Bomber Harris's boys were now pulverising it without mercy.

When dawn came, our train cautiously crawled its way into the city, as if it were treading on eggshells. We began to see the devastation our own side had wreaked on Nuremberg. Jagged, blackened fragments of buildings stuck up in the air like burnt toast. On a fine August morning, a fog of smoke from still-raging fires hung over the streets and squares. Inside the station, a worse sight was waiting.

At one of the platforms stood the train we had tried to board at Augsburg the night before. Or what was left of it. It had pulled into the station just as the air raid began and received a direct hit. It seemed that after they'd dropped their bomb, the pilots had then circled back and machine-gunned it. Not a soul had escaped alive. The train had become a mass grave. All the German and Italian soldiers we'd seen last night, laughing and joking as they'd squeezed into the carriages, now lay inside, dead. If Tony and I had been in the guard's van, we'd have copped it, too.

We stared at the burnt-out wreck as the fire and ambulance crews began to remove the charred bodies. Christ, that could have been us. But it wasn't. And all because a station master, a stickler for the rules, whose name we would never know, had refused to let us board it. On such bizarre twists of fate your life could depend. Heinrich, Tony and I walked away from the horror of it in silence, our heads down. What words could there be?

To continue our onward journey we had to cross the centre of the city to another terminus. The destruction was hard to look at; ambulances were everywhere. Men, women and children stood in quiet groups, stunned and silent. Bloody bandages were wrapped round heads, arms and legs. God knows how many people had been killed or injured. You had to really force yourself to remember the carnage the Germans had done to London, Bristol, Coventry and other places back home. But I wished now I'd never hoped the RAF would pull their socks up. It was impossible to feel any sense of triumph, only sadness and regret at the waste of it all. These were terrible things for people to do to one another.

'Don't let anyone hear you speaking English,' said Heinrich, 'or they might well lynch you.'

With this in mind, he kept his gun in his pocket as we crossed the city so that we wouldn't be identified as POWs. It was a decent gesture and we were grateful for it.

We made our way along a street towards the station. The pavements were strewn with rubble from last night's bombing. As everywhere else, there were small sad clumps of people standing around or sitting on piles of dusty, broken bricks; some talking quietly, some weeping with their heads in their hands. Every now and then, the sound of ambulance sirens cut through the smoky air.

When we reached the other station, we discovered that the train we had been due to take had been bombed and machine gunned just like the one from Augsburg. Again, we had to sit and wait for yet another train. By now, I felt I could write a travel guide to the railway stations of Germany.

Eventually, stage by stage, Happy Heinrich delivered us safely to Stalag XXA. I don't think a soldier had ever been happier to see the end of a mission than that bloke was. I imagined him back in his barracks, telling his pals about these two 'desperate characters' he'd dragged back all the way across Germany through the horrors of war.

When the great gates of Fort 13 rose up in front of us again, we got a splendid welcome. All the lads were at the windows. I soon spotted Sam Kydd and gave him a wave. Though they were all sad for us, they cheered and applauded as Tony and I marched back across the drawbridge. I didn't know whether to laugh or cry. It wasn't much more than a week since we'd left. In that short time, we'd seen Berlin, dined in a grand hotel, enjoyed a lager in Adolf's famous beer cellar and breathed in the fresh, free air from the Alps. We'd also come very close to being executed as spies. It had been a busy week.

The Commandant himself, an old-school Prussian officer, came out to meet us. Quite an honour. He couldn't believe we'd managed to get as far as the Swiss border in just forty-eight hours.

'My congratulations gentlemen, it is the best escape plan I have yet seen in Stalag XXA,' he said. 'You deserved to have succeeded. Unfortunately, I am not allowed to let you off completely.'

To do them justice, the German authorities always accepted that it was a prisoner's right to try to escape. We were all soldiers and there was a definite professional admiration from the Jerries that we'd dreamed up such a bold plan and got within a whisker of carrying it off. And the punishment was relatively light. We would spend just two weeks in the 'cooler' with the rats. Nasty though it was, both Tony and I had been through it before. We'd survive. At least we would be together in there.

We had other companions, too: among them Willie and Fergus who were still paying the price for having helped us escape. Being shoved in through the door of the cooler and coming face to face with the two grooms was probably the toughest thing about coming back to Fort 13. The sacrifices they'd made for Tony and me had been in vain.

'Well, lads,' said Willie, looking up. 'How was your wee break? Did you have nice weather?'

But they couldn't quite hide the sadness we saw in their faces. Still it was good to have them beside us in the cooler. It forced Tony and me to put on a brave face, to laugh and joke our way through the aching disappointment we were both feeling.

Naturally, Willie and Fergus wanted to hear all about it. Tony and I spun them all the tales of our days on the run. How we'd failed to pick up a tart in Berlin. How we'd had that splendid lunch surrounded by German officers. How the bits of torn-up paper had nearly swum over the top of the Gestapo lavatory in Lindau. The darker stuff, being knocked about by the Jerries, all the death and destruction we'd witnessed, we kept to ourselves.

'Well, it sounds like you got pretty close,' said Fergus. 'Not a bad try for two Englishmen.'

A few days later, I was allowed at last to write a letter to Peggy. I confessed that I'd been banged up for an attempted escape. But as with the grooms, I never told her the worst parts of it. Maybe I'd tell her one day in the distant future, but in the meantime, I did my best to make it sound as if Tony and I had just taken a little summer holiday. I was as fit as a fiddle, I wrote. No need to worry her pretty red head about me. I was fine.

But I wasn't. It was going to be Peg's birthday in a few weeks and I'd been determined that I'd hold her in my arms on that day. I'd pictured us walking along the riverbank at Barnard Castle, hand in hand, starting out all over again. After only five weeks as man and wife, she'd had to wait patiently for me for two and a half years, her life in a sort of limbo. I'd never wanted her to have another birthday without me as long as she lived. But that was going to happen now and it hurt like hell.

Outside, in the prisoners' vegetable patches and flowerbeds, were the first signs of the end of summer. Autumn would soon come, then the Polish winter, when the ceilings of our sleeping quarters would drip with damp, the days would become short and cheerless, the nights numbingly cold. How much longer would we all have to be prisoners? How much more captivity could the human spirit take? Would this fucking war never end? Surely, it must do some time? But when would that be? I was the resilient sort alright; I knew that. Damned if Adolf Hitler was going to break Fred Foster. But how many bouts of barbed wire fever could you drag yourself through without going just a bit doolally? I didn't know the answer to a single one of all these questions.

But it turned out that I was never to spend another winter in Fort 13, not even an autumn. One day, towards the end of our time in the 'cooler', a guard came in to our dark, smelly cell.

'Foster, come with me,' he said.

'Why?'

'The Commandant wishes to see you,' he replied.

'Why?' I repeated.

'You are to be moved,' he said. 'You are leaving Stalag XXA.'

And so I was. The Jerries had decided now to move senior NCOs out of this and other 'working' camps and transfer the whole bloody lot of us to some new place in Bavaria. Ironically, the very area I'd only just returned from.

It all happened so fast. I was given precious little time to gather my personal bits and pieces together before the truck arrived to take us to the station at Torun. The same place Tony and I had set out from a couple of weeks before, in our smart new suits, full of hope, heading for home.

I said my goodbyes to special mates like Sam Kydd and Jimmy Woolcock, very much hoping that we'd meet again back home when all of this was over. Then I was allowed five minutes to go back to the 'cooler'.

'Well then Freddie,' said Tony with a big smile.' You're getting out of here after all.'

'Looks like it,' I said.

I was suddenly shy, an emotion not often associated with Fred Foster. Embarrassed, too. I hardly knew what words to use and only feeble ones came out. He had never abandoned me and now it felt as if I were abandoning him. We were close as comrades could be. We had faced death together in a Nazi prison. But still neither could say to the other how much the other meant to him. All we could use was the language of Englishmen like ourselves. The understated expressions. The stiff upper lip. Our deepest feelings held firmly in check.

'We had a good run, didn't we?' said Tony.

'We certainly did.'

'Well, I'll be seeing you, as the song goes.'

'Yes indeed,' I smiled as we shook each other's hand. 'Be seeing you, Tony.'

But that wouldn't happen. I would never see Tony Coulthard alive again.

PART THREE

LOST AND FOUND

CHAPTER ELEVEN

Freedom, that state for which they both so yearned, would eventually come to Antony Coulthard and Fred Foster. But they would find it in very different ways and it would be a long time coming.

The 'glorious, successful, heartbreaking failure' of their escape attempt from Stalag XXA took place at almost exactly the halfway point of their captivity during World War Two. In the end, they were both destined to be prisoners of the Third Reich for just under five years.

*

Fred was transported south-west across Germany to Stalag 383 at Hohenfels in Bavaria, an isolated location about fifty miles north-east of Munich. Until recently, this had been a camp for officers but it was now to house senior NCOs who, under the terms of the Geneva Convention, were not required to work. In camps like Stalag XXA at Torun, the Germans had brazenly flouted this regulation, but by the autumn of 1942 they had agreed to respect it and NCOs from all over Germany and Poland were transferred to Stalag 383. Within a few months, it housed nearly six thousand men.

When Fred Foster arrived, he found a camp that was different in many ways from his Polish prison. Instead of the dank, overcrowded old forts of Stalag XXA, here were row upon row of wooden chalets, each one holding no more than a dozen or so men. Instead of the close proximity of a large town like Torun, his new home was out in the countryside, several miles from any civilian population. It stood in a large clearing surrounded by thick pine forests, which allowed the prisoners plenty of room for sports and a welcome sense of space, but perhaps increased a sense of exile from the outside world.

One thing that remained the same was the freezing temperatures of the central European winter. Even the Germans referred to this corner of Bavaria as 'the Siberia of Deutschland'. Each chalet was fitted with a stove and there was no shortage of wood from the surrounding forests, but the huts were still ice boxes for several months of the year. Freed from the necessity to work (which was a mixed blessing), many prisoners often stayed in bed, fully clothed in greatcoat, balaclava and mittens, for long parts of the winter day.

So, though on balance Fred Foster must have been glad to be moved, his essential situation hadn't changed. He was still a prisoner and no nearer getting home to Peggy.

To increase his anxiety, the move to a new camp had disrupted the mail from home and it was more than a month before anything like regularity was resumed. But one of the earliest letters to reach him cheered him hugely. Peggy announced that she, too, was to move, leaving her life-long home in Barnard Castle to live at 32 Bowbridge Road, Newark, with Fred's father, Harry the bricklayer, and his sister Hilda to whom she had become very attached. She was Mrs Foster after all, part of that family, and she had now decided that was where she ought to be.

'That is the best news I have had for a long time,' he wrote and then confesses, 'I have quite got over my other disappointment now, but for weeks I was stunned and terribly disappointed. We were so near to success.'

Fred's basic nature, with its ability to make the best of whatever came his way, reasserted itself. Once again, he picked up his studies, investing in the prosperous future he was determined he and Peggy were going to have. And he was laying plans for it. The builder's business Harry's brothers had set up had done surprisingly well and become quite a large concern. Aware of Fred's sharp mind and clerical skills, his uncles had offered him a role when he returned from the war and Fred intended to take it: the next step up the ladder.

'I haven't had room to tell you before, but I sat an examination in advanced economics as well as a teacher's diploma in shorthand,' he wrote. 'I shan't know the result for a few months, but I'm very confident.'

The usual POW recreations soon got going, too. The football, the rugby, the boxing. The concerts, the variety shows, the productions of Gilbert & Sullivan. The scenery might have changed but the daily life of prisoners of war carried on much as it had in Poland. The letters that came for him weren't just from Peggy, Hilda, Harry and his friends back home. They also came from Fort 13. From Sam Kydd and Jimmy Woolcock. And from Antony, too, always cheerful, always positive.

But that first Christmas in Stalag 383 was tough. He had been so sure he would be home again. In his mind, he kept going over his bid for freedom with Antony.

'When my reunion with you seemed so certain, my heart was full to overflowing, because I thought your long vigil had ended,' he wrote to his wife in his last letter before Christmas. 'And when I was paying the penalty for failure, your dear presence permeated through the window of my cell and then my troubled mind was soothed and calm.'

He worried terribly that she was going to a new job in Newark, at a munitions factory called Ransome and Marles. His concern was not unfounded. In March 1941, it had been bombed in broad daylight, killing over forty workers and injuring more than one hundred and fifty. It was the blackest day of Newark's war. By now, few places in Britain dared ever boast that they were safe from the Luftwaffe. Even if the actual target had been a large town or city nearby, the Germans might still unload their remaining bombs anywhere, in order to get home faster. Fred was arguably safer in a camp in Bavaria than Peggy was on the streets of Nottinghamshire.

Life for Fred's wife can hardly have been comfortable in the tiny house in Bowbridge Road. She and Hilda would have shared a cramped bedroom, with Harry in the other. The only lavatory was still outside in a lean-to; the single tap in the kitchen sink still only gave cold water. Long, blacked-out winter evenings can't have been much fun in the little sitting-room at the back, the air thick with Harry's cigarette smoke, listening to Tommy Handley or Flanagan and Allen on the wireless. Once a week she and Hilda might visit the pictures, but it's unlikely she would have gone to the local dance hall and put herself into the arms of any randy soldier on leave. Too many married women had done that, with tragic consequences nine months later. Peggy Foster was made of sterner stuff. She joined the Civil Defence instead.

So why did Fred Foster, the man who'd got so close to freedom, wait for almost another two and a half years before he made another attempt to escape? Like Antony Coulthard, he was one of those whose natures baulked against the very concept of captivity. Still completely in thrall to his passion for his wife, he was obsessed with getting home to her. What took him so long?

There could be several reasons. First, Stalag 383 was adjacent to a military training ground, its layout more regimented and much more tricky to get out of than Stalag XXA, with its old buildings and scattered geography full of shady corners and other places to hide. With a double row of lethal barbed wire and high watchtowers all around it, the Germans boasted that it was a 'cast-iron' camp. Secondly, even if he'd got through the wire, he'd have been easily spotted in an area filled with the military, antagonistic enemy civilians and no sympathetic local underground that could supply him with vital papers, money and clothing. Third, he must have realised that the war, especially after El Alamein in 1942, was at long last tilting towards an Allied victory. Fred was a member of the camp's secret radio team and would have had an accurate fix, via the BBC, of what was happening far beyond the wire. In the summer of 1944, the Allies had landed in Normandy. By that winter, they had reached Germany's western border and the Russian Red Army had now made inroads into Poland and eastern Prussia. Fred may well have come to the conclusion that he had a better chance of staying alive by staying put. Surely, it couldn't be long now.

'Sweetheart, do you realise that this is the last winter you're going to have the hot water bottle all to yourself in bed?' he wrote just before Christmas.

But the Allied advances were the silver lining of a very dark cloud. The steady decline in the Nazis' fortunes was soon reflected in daily life at Stalag 383. The tolerable comfort in which the POWs had been living for the previous two years began to erode fast and, in a remarkably short time, conditions became no better than those Fred had left behind in Poland. As the Third Reich began to split at the seams, so did the support structures for their prisoners of war.

Crucially, the tireless efforts of the Red Cross, 'that watchful second mother to us all' as one POW gratefully put it, were more and more hampered. Fewer of the precious parcels got through and, when they did, they had to be shared among a larger number of men. It had now become far harder to get hold of the basic necessities. Fred wrote that his clothing and possessions had dwindled. Personal hygiene became tricky, too, with increasing problems in getting razor blades, toothpaste and soap.

'It gets a bit embarrassing at times,' he wrote, putting it as delicately as possible.

Worst of all, basic food supplies to the camp were getting ever more sparse, even for their German captors. Many men were several stone underweight and dozens blacked out every day at morning roll call. During the winter of 1944/5, the cold seemed to be worse than ever, gnawing into your bones no matter how many layers you wrapped yourself in. One man who'd created a wolf-skin as a pantomime costume for a production of *Red Riding Hood* now wore it daily to help keep him warm.

'In his present half-starved condition,' wrote one friend in a diary, 'he doesn't need the skin on to look like a wolf.'

But by now there were no more amateur dramatics. The sports pitches were rock hard and unusable, even if anyone had the energy or the inclination. The prisoners stayed in their huts, immured in boredom.

It was so cold that a table, wiped down with a damp cloth, would be frozen over in no time. The stove, even when alight, often had a layer of thin ice on top of it. And, for some reason no longer clear, fuel became ever harder to come by. Maybe the Germans just refused to cut down any more trees, but the effect was dire. The men started burning anything they could lay their hands on; wooden boards from their bunks, even beams from the ceiling, which made the roof sag and let the wind whistle in through crevices where the supports had been removed. In one hut, their only table had to be suspended on ropes from the roof because they had burnt the table legs. But one prisoner described the intense pleasure he gained in burning a copy of Hitler's *Mein Kampf*, which Goebbels had ordered to be sent to the camp library, and watching it crinkle up and disintegrate. It was a small payback for the infamous book-burning of the Nazi barbarians in the 1930s.

In this situation, it wasn't surprising that tempers frayed more easily and solidarity with your comrades became harder to sustain. Even close friends could fall out over some tiny, imagined misdemeanour.

'Insults are batted about like shuttlecocks,' wrote the diarist. 'Families, regiments and religions are all dragged in, but there are no fights. No one's got the energy and even the dimmest realise that words just now mean nothing.'

But there was one benefit to be found in the bickering.

'Unintelligible as the squabbling might be to an outsider, ignoble as it seems to ourselves, it serves to stem off apathy. Better to argue about it than to lie all day and mope. That way, madness lies. And the row's soon over anyway. Someone makes a crack, somebody else laughs, nerves relax all round.'

In that last grim winter, next to the curse of the cold, it was their ever-growing hunger that tested the spirits of the prisoners.

'It's still about the grub,' wrote the diarist. 'Nothing else quite registers. But it's now wistful reminiscences of mother's puddings or starry-eyed eulogies of the wife's pancakes.'

Thankfully, the news that came through on their underground radios was definitely nourishing to the spirit. Almost by the day, the conviction was fed that World War Two would soon be over.

'Next year will be a great one,' Fred promised Peggy. 'I know it will see all of our hopes realised and our dreams come true.'

If the camp censors took any offence at the implications of that sentence, they didn't strike it out. Perhaps by now they could see little point in the job they were doing.

Then, incredibly, just weeks before the war was over, Fred Foster did indeed try to escape again. The answer for this apparently bizarre action seems to have been self-preservation. The Americans were advancing fast. The Senior British Officer had asked for volunteers to attempt escape from the camp, make contact with the Yanks and let them know of its existence so that they wouldn't bombard it from the air. The exact details of Fred's second adventure, in March 1945, are unclear, but it seems he wasn't one of those who made it out. Second time unlucky. But in these febrile, complex circumstances, perhaps the opposite was the truth.

Soon afterwards, on 23 March, Fred sent one last, confident letter home to 32 Bowbridge Road.

'Well that's my thirtieth birthday finished and my last away from you. It hasn't been a bad one really darling because two lorries suddenly arrived with enough Red Cross parcels for half a parcel a man, so we eat once again! I can't imagine a life where one doesn't have to worry about tomorrow's food, but it's near.'

And it was. A few weeks later, on 1 May 1945, the Americans liberated Stalag 383 and, after five years as a POW, Sergeant Fred Foster had his freedom. He was going home to Peggy.

The day before, the Allies had reached central Berlin. Their soldiers marched down Unter den Linden, where Fred and Antony had strolled in those new suits a couple of years earlier. Deep in his bunker underneath The Chancellery, Adolf Hitler gave his new bride Eva Braun a cyanide capsule then put a pistol to his head. It was all over.

*

But what of Antony?

Back in August 1942, after Fred had been removed from the 'cooler' in Fort 13 and his own sentence had been served, Antony went back to the life he had known before. Now though, his card was yet more heavily marked than ever. He was one to be watched. A judgement with which it was hard to argue.

And the Germans were quite right. Because Lance Corporal Coulthard went on to become one of the most persistent escapers of World War Two. Far from being dispirited by the failure of his attempt with Fred Foster, the opposite seems to have occurred. Though military intelligence records are not entirely clear, it is possible that he tried for freedom no less than a further *eight* times.

Despite how close he and Fred had come to success, Antony never again tried the route to Switzerland. In late 1943, in the most prominent of his subsequent escape attempts, he and Sergeant Neil McLellan reverted to the well-trodden route to the Baltic Coast in the hope of a ship to neutral Sweden. Yet again, they got as close to pulling it off as it was possible to get. This time, they'd managed to reach the port of Gydnia and actually been able to board a ship, stowing away in the stokehold till the ship set sail. Then the usual curse of the Baltic route claimed them. For the umpteenth time, an Italian dockworker, in the pay of the Gestapo, betrayed them to the port authorities. Back they went to Fort 13. To the cheers, the applause and the 'cooler'.

As Antony's escape attempts piled up, the Germans lost the admiration for his pluck that they had expressed when he and Fred had marched back in through the gates in August 1942. Coulthard was beginning to make them look like fools and the proud Germans really couldn't have that. Though still nominally attached to Stalag XXA, he was now exiled from his friends, condemned to hard labour and sent to a disciplinary camp to the north of Torun.

The work was tough physically, but the slightly built 'Professor', the boy who'd spent most of his life in libraries, never did less than his share. He was even proud to be among a body of men classified by the Germans as 'habitual nuisances and escapees'.

Among the Germans, however, were still some officers who quietly respected the terrier-like tenacity of his attempts to break free, who did not want him unduly persecuted and who were quite willing that he should return to Fort 13 and resume the useful roles he'd performed there. For some time though, he seems to have been a victim of the tensions that existed between different departments of the German Army. By 1944, the *Arbeitseinsatz,* the authority that directed the treatment of POWs, wielded a great deal of power and was staffed by some of the most vicious soldiers in the Third Reich. Perhaps intimidated by Antony's intelligence and spirit, not to mention his record, some of them set out to target him, hoping to goad him into retaliating and giving them an excuse for violence against him. Hitler's cronies never succeeded in that, but letters to his parents described the severity of the conditions, the dreadful food and how tired he always felt these days. Luckily, as time passed, the kinder of the Stalag authorities decided there was no longer any reason to keep him in a disciplinary camp and he was allowed back to Fort 13 on health grounds.

He would have been glad to see his old comrades again, but not as glad as they were to see the same old 'Prof' behind his grubby glasses, still regaling them of an evening with the stories of his nine escape attempts, especially the first one with 'good old Freddie Foster'. How excruciating Fred's German accent had been. How on the train he, Tony, had dozed on top of the suitcase filled with butter and eggs and ruined the lot. And the now well-worn anecdote of how he and Fred had failed to pick up a tart in Berlin. Were we really so unattractive, do you think?

'My last memory of the Prof is the sight of him sitting on a box in a cold room with a 25-watt lamp,' wrote the camp Padre afterwards, 'with deep concern for the whereabouts of one of his friends wanted by the Gestapo for working with the Polish partisans. Offering his wise comments, criticisms and suggestions to bring him back into the safety of the Stalag.'

But Antony's health was creating more cause for concern. By now, he was showing the early signs of tuberculosis. But, as in Fred Foster's camp far off in Bavaria, the inmates of Stalag XXA were suffused with greater hope than they had dared to feel in nearly five years. Many were convinced that, by the same time next year, they would have picked up the threads of their lives again. They would stop being just names, ranks and numbers. Once again, they would be the butcher, the baker, the farmer, the factory worker. Or the brilliant young linguist destined for the Foreign Office.

That hope was tragically premature. The Allied POWs were about to be swept up in one of the worst humanitarian crimes of World War Two. In January 1945, as the Red Army advanced from the east, the Nazis committed a last spectacular piece of cruelty against their fellow men.

Seventy years later, historians still do not agree on the Germans' purpose in emptying all their eastern POW camps, but the order seems to have come from the highest levels in Berlin, probably from Adolf Hitler himself. Some think that his aim was to use the prisoners as bargaining chips to negotiate a last-minute peace settlement with the Allies. Or perhaps it was just one last spasm of Nazi rage against the enemies who were about to consign the Third Reich to the cesspit of history. Whatever the truth of it, instead of simply leaving the prisoners in the camps to await their imminent liberation, The Führer decreed that they should be marched westwards, away from the encroaching Soviets.

On 21 January, the POWs of Stalag XXA were given twelve hours' notice to gather their belongings and evacuate the camp. There were around six hundred British and over a thousand Russians. In those twelve hours, fear spread through the camp, wiping out the high hopes all of them had that their captivity might very soon be over. What the hell was going on? The most frightening possibility was that they were being led to concentration camps to be exterminated in revenge for the recent carpet-bombing of German cities by the British and American air forces.

What became known to history as the Forced Marches had begun. Over eighty thousand prisoners, in various small columns like Antony's, now embarked on a trek across Poland and Germany in one of the worst winters in living memory. They were allowed to carry three days' rations and thirty pounds of kit. All Red Cross parcels were to be handed in; these would be carried in a wagon. The daily ration for each man would be three hundred grams of bread and twenty-five grams of margarine. But after only a couple of days, these supplies ran out and for the next three weeks each man survived on nothing more than four steamed potatoes a day. The Red Cross parcels in the wagons were now being pilfered by the German guards and there was precious little sustenance to be found there.

Thick snow blanketed the ground and temperatures sank to 25F below zero. Regardless of their medical condition, the men were expected to cover up to forty-five kilometres a day. In reality, the going was usually at a snail's pace and these pathetic, straggling columns would be wandering across the frozen plains of northern Europe for the best part of the next three months. Exact casualty figures do not exist, but it is estimated that somewhere between three and eight thousand men died in the misery of disease and starvation. It was the Nazis' last horrible hurrah.

The majority of the prisoners were already weakened through years of a poor diet. There was little or no shelter from the intense cold; nights were spent in unheated barns along the way. Their clothing, in most cases the battle dress in which they had been captured five years before, was totally inadequate for the hellish conditions they faced. As time passed, their food was mostly raw vegetables foraged from the fields. The limited drinking water available on the march was sometimes dubious and many contracted dysentery, if they didn't have it already. As usual, many men were infested with lice. Their discomfort and desolation must have been indescribable.

Antony's column numbered around six hundred men. The officer in charge of it was called Hauptmann (Captain) Mackensen, a man of exceptional cruelty. A pharmacist in civilian life, he had been so perverted by Nazi ideology that it seemed his purpose was no longer to make people better but to make them suffer as much as possible. Over several years, his reputation among the POWs in Poland had grown ever more grim. This was a man who had allowed escaped prisoners to be shot in the back after they had surrendered.

Now, as the Forced March began, Mackensen had instructed his guards not to allow any stragglers. As they crossed empty countryside, there were simply no facilities for the sick to 'fall out', nor any transport to take them to medical help. Whoever fell by the wayside was to be shot, bayonetted or beaten to death. The prisoners had a simple choice: walk or die. Mackensen himself rode at the head of the column on a sledge pulled by a pony. He seldom looked back at the horror that was swiftly developing behind him. Anyway, he believed that most of those who claimed they couldn't go on were merely malingering.

On 11 February, as the column crossed a desolate plain, a fierce blizzard tore into them. Many of the prisoners developed severe frostbite which, with no medical supplies whatever, was left untreated and would eventually lead to the amputation of feet, toes and fingers. There was no German or British doctor permanently attached to the column; only an irregular flying visit by four or five itinerant Nazi doctors, who could do precious little for a group of no fewer than six hundred suffering men.

At one point, a large supply of Red Cross parcels lay only ten miles away from the route of the march: the prisoners knew this because they had seen these being transported past them. Staff Sergeant Thomas Aitken, one of the senior British NCOs on the march, asked Mackensen to allow a small party of men to break off and collect some of these, but he refused without giving any reason whatsoever.

There were no deaths until about one month into the Forced March, but gradually, as the prisoners grew weaker, the fatalities snowballed, mostly from hunger and dysentery but some from the brutality of the guards. Sergeant Aitken fought to be allowed to make arrangements with the *Bürgermeisters* (the mayors) of nearby villages and towns for these fatalities to be registered and for the erection of a simple wooden cross with the dead man's name on it.

The column marched slowly west across northern Poland and into Germany, moving just inland from the Baltic coast, past the old towns of Gustrow and Schwerin. By early March, after six weeks on the move, Antony Coulthard was in a very poor state. There had been a slight improvement in food supplies to the column; they were now about the acceptable level for a day's ration back in Stalag XXA, but were still hopelessly inadequate for seriously weakened men who were expected to walk many kilometres every day. Certainly, the improvement could do little for the nearly broken body of Antony Coulthard. Still, however, he tried to act as an interpreter for others and, like Sergeant Aitken, as a spokesman in trying to secure better conditions and treatment – a role that hardly improved his popularity with the guards.

The Germans were not entirely without scruples. At one point, it was decided that the march could pause for several days. Thanks to the constant pressure by Sergeant Thomas Aitken, Antony was one of those permitted to be taken into a nearby hospital, suffering from severe dysentery. The comfort of a decent bed and a reasonable amount of food must have been beyond belief. But after a few days, the march moved on and only the very serious cases were left behind. Anyone able to stand was considered fit enough to continue. And Antony, dragging himself from his bed, was just about able to achieve that. How one wishes he had been able to remain there. If only he had pretended to be sicker than he was, though God knows he was sick enough. But that would not have been his way. His bed could be used for someone in even greater need than him, so he must let them have it. On 12 March, he walked out of his last refuge and staggered on.

Eventually the column reached a location about sixty kilometres from Hamburg. Here, there may have been another brief flicker of humanity from Hauptmann Mackensen and his men. Or perhaps they just realised that some prisoners, though still walking, simply could not move any faster. Antony and the other sickest prisoners were now allowed to travel in a rickety cart. He would survive the carts, but many others died around him. All of Sergeant Aitken's pleas for further medical help were turned down.

But even the small mercy of the carts was soon negated by the arrival of a new set of guards, who turned out to be even harsher than the previous crew.

'The worst crowd we had met so far,' remembered one man afterwards. 'We told them we were sick men, but they ill-treated us more than ever and frequently hit us with their fists and rifle butts.'

After sixty days of marching, ever more exhausted, hungry and miserable, Antony's column reached the small town of Dömitz on the banks of the River Elbe in Lower Saxony. They had now walked over one thousand miles, an unbelievable feat for men in their condition. Of the six hundred or so in Antony's column who had set out on the Forced March, only about half that number now remained. Most of the men who had escaped from the column under cover of darkness and set out across the snow with no food could be presumed to have died of exposure; their bodies hidden under its crisp white blanket till the spring thaw would lay them bare.

By the time the column stopped at Dömitz, there were a further twenty-nine shallow graves marking the route they had taken from Poland. Antony was now in terrible condition. Weak as a baby, not only from dysentery but now also from the tuberculosis, which was slowly filling his lungs. There was only so much resilience the human body could muster and Antony Coulthard's was running out fast.

Yet, as he had done throughout his young life, he put others before himself. On several occasions, he was seen giving his small portion of food to other comrades who needed it more. That is what his God would have wanted him to do. That was how John and Dorothy Coulthard had raised him. So that was what he did.

Hauptmann Mackensen had turned the column towards Dömitz for a reason. On the flat countryside on the west bank of the Elbe, opposite the town, was a scattered group of farms and hamlets. At one of these, called Kaltenhof, a local Nazi military headquarters had been set up. For two nights, the prisoners were to stop here: a merciful breathing space in their endless ordeal. A large barn had been requisitioned to provide some shelter, but there was to be a price to pay for such unaccustomed luxury. The frail, hungry men were now forced into the freezing waters of the River Elbe, in an attempt to wash away the scourge of lice and the soilings of dysentery. Some men almost welcomed this unexpected bath, but for those like Antony who were desperately ill, it must have been one more torture.

When he staggered out of the heart-stopping water, he lost consciousness and was carried back to the barn by his friends. They laid him on the earth-floor, tried to warm him up and make him as comfortable as possible. Beyond that, there was nothing to be done except to return to him the kindness and concern he had always shown to each and every one of them.

Despite the generous size of the barn, the prisoners were jammed in tightly and Antony now lay between two of his comrades as twilight fell and the barn sank into darkness.

Antony Coulthard had now reached a frontier over which he had no choice but to cross and this time there could be no turning back. In the early hours of 24 March 1945, a fortnight before his twenty-seventh birthday, he crossed it. His body had long since had enough and now his spirit gave up, too.

But how tragic was the timing. Spring was just beginning to push its way up through the earth; the days were growing longer and the sun a little warmer. The end of the damned war, which had torn the world apart, was getting closer with every dawn. Less than three weeks after Antony's death, his sad column of prisoners was liberated by the approaching Americans. It seemed to be his recurring destiny to almost get to freedom, but to never quite make it. In another sense, of course, he had now done just that.

As he lay that night in the darkened barn, his life ebbing away, it is to be hoped that some happy thoughts comforted him. Of his parents and sisters in the Villa Vita. Of his old friends on the staircases and quadrangles of Oxford. Of the men with whom he'd lived for the last five years, in a situation none of them had ever imagined they might encounter, but with which they had coped with guts and good humour. And none more so than 'The Professor', the geeky boy in the horn-rimmed glasses who, when faced with the very worst that could happen, drew out of himself the very best and used it to touch and illuminate the lives of those around him. It was a young life cut short and it breaks the heart to imagine what he might otherwise have done with it. But nobody who ever knew him would have called it 'wasted'.

CHAPTER TWELVE

She heard his boots first. Coming down the outside passageway that led from the street to the door of 32 Bowbridge Road. She was used to hearing steps in the passageway: the neighbours, the coalman, the milkman. Harry, of course, and Hilda. In the two and a half years she'd shared the little house with her husband's family, Peggy had learned to recognise their different footfalls. At first, she couldn't place the heavy steps she heard on this quiet May evening. Then she did and she thought her heart would burst open. It was Fred.

When she flung the door wide open, there he was. Still in his battle-dress. Carrying a little suitcase. Older of course than she remembered him. And so much thinner. But it was her Fred alright.

She'd known he was coming, just not exactly when. The information on returning POWs was sketchy and confusing; there were tens of thousands of men rushing home and bureaucracy just couldn't cope. She'd already been down to Newark station twice that day, standing on tiptoe on the platform, trying to catch sight of him above the heads of the madding crowd, her pulse racing, excited and nervous at one and the same time. She'd put on one of her nicest frocks and done her hair and make-up. She'd kept a slight smile poised at the corners of her mouth, all ready to break into a wild grin at the first sight of him. But both times she'd eventually had to sigh, give up and push her way out through the cries and shouts and the frantic waves of people who'd been luckier than she had been.

Chapter Twelve

But none of that mattered now. There was pandemonium on the doorstep of the bricklayer's house. Harry and Hilda. Hugs and kisses. Floods of tears and gales of laughter. Years of worry and despair dissolved in the joy of his deliverance. No more letters need ever be written; everything they felt could now be spoken. It *was* just like in the films. Happy endings did happen after all.

That Fred's return was deliriously happy for them all is without a doubt. What is also certain is that it was not free from difficulty. He and Peggy had only known each other for five months before their wedding, been married for just five weeks before he left for Norway and been apart for nearly five years. With the best will in the world, neither of them was quite the same person he or she had been before. Like tens of millions of others all over the world, they had lived through a cataclysm and were not unscathed by it. For Fred, of course, it was worse; he had known hunger, cold and misery. He had seen comrades killed all around him and come dangerously close to death himself.

But Peggy, too, was not exactly the girl she had been on the steps of St Mary's Church on her wedding day. Since then, she had been forced to deal with circumstances and emotions with which no young woman should have to cope. But there was something else, too. For large numbers of British women, the war had also been a kind of liberation, however temporary, from the prison of conventional domesticity. Even if they hadn't joined the ATS or the Women's Land Army, they may have worked in factories, as Peggy had, or in myriad other roles that, without the war, would have been firmly closed to them. When the war was over, many of these women, their self-confidence and self-respect boosted as never before, were reluctant to revert to the way things had been. In many relationships, the return of the hero brought tensions as well as joy. When they reached home, many soldiers discovered that they had to rethink their attitudes to what had often been called the 'gentler sex'. There was no shortage of women who had proved themselves every bit as tough as their menfolk and, in some ways, far tougher. Any woman who had had to raise her children alone, to feed and clothe them in times of shortages and rationing, not to mention the threat of bombing, had fought a long, hard battle of her own.

So now Fred and Peggy had to get to know each other all over again. Despite the intensity of their wartime letters, being in each other's physical presence again was not without shyness and nerves on both sides. One of Fred's letters home had hinted at the possibility that his new bride, so achingly young, had lost her nerve on the wedding night and the marriage had still not been consummated when he had left for the war. So that hurdle was waiting to be taken once again. Nor could living in extreme proximity with Harry and Hilda have given the reunited couple much privacy. Walls were thin.

There were other hurdles, too. Behind his usual cheery exterior, Fred was not entirely 'home' again. In some ways, his mindset was still in the prison camp. Peggy would later talk of how strange his behaviour had been in those first months. She would sometimes find scraps of food ferreted away in odd places: a biscuit in the linen cupboard, a piece of cheese under the mattress. The man who for five years had rarely been sure where his next meal might come from couldn't bear to see anything go to waste.

Today, such behaviour would be recognised as a symptom of Post Traumatic Stress Disorder. Luckily, even back in 1945, it was understood that many troops returning home, from either conflict or captivity, wouldn't find it easy to pick up the reins of their old lives as if they had never been away and the war nothing more than a bad dream. Families were sent a leaflet warning them of the difficulties and adjustments that might lie ahead. In the middle of the night, plenty of young wives were woken by the sweat-soaked nightmares of the soldiers who had returned to lie beside them. It would take a lot of love, patience and understanding.

Thankfully, Peggy Foster had plenty of that to give, because her husband was about to need it. World War Two had not finished raining down its blows on Fred Foster. One of the biggest was about to hit him.

Little more than week after Fred reached home, the postman's familiar step was heard coming down the passageway. The letter that landed on the mat carried a Hampshire postmark. Its contents were to devastate the recipient and its effect would never leave him.

'Dear Sergeant Foster,' wrote Mrs. Dorothy Coulthard, 'I suppose you know that my son, or 'The Professor', from Stalag XXA, perished on the way home on one of those torture marches from Poland. Corporal AG Price, who lives in this district, managed to get your address, hence this letter. I would particularly have liked to see you, as I believe you were the co-escapee with my son to the Swiss border in 1942 and, from what I have heard, he made the fatal mistake of returning to help you at the last moment; foolhardy but praiseworthy! And now he has gone, perished miserably and unnecessarily!'

But Dorothy Coulthard was mistaken. Fred Foster did not know that his old chum was dead and the shock was immense.

'Four of his closest friends (one wrote to me on his arrival home) buried Antony in a little civilian cemetery at Dömitz. They asked a passing German civilian to put up a rough wooden cross bearing his name, rank and number, as the march had to go on. As soon as I can, I shall visit this hallowed spot – the only one in all Germany for me. He was my idol, I just worshipped him and I am broken-hearted. To the end of my days this wound will never heal...'

When Fred Foster reread the letter, as he surely did, for the second, third or fourth time, it would surely have been that one sentence that echoed in his ears.

'He made the fatal mistake of returning to help you.'

In any letter, especially one between strangers, it can be difficult to 'hear the voice' of the person who wrote it. In that echoing sentence, was Dorothy Coulthard's voice merely resigned and sad, or was there anger and recrimination, too? As she put down the words was there just a lump in her throat, or fury in her breast? How could Fred Foster ever know?

He replied at once, trying to find compassionate heartfelt words for a distraught mother, without overstepping the mark into a familiarity that might have been unwelcome.

'A truly gallant fellow, a good comrade and a very dear personal friend,' he wrote. 'He was liked, even beloved, by everyone with whom he came in contact.'

Dorothy Coulthard had asked to know the full story of the escape attempt of 1942 and Fred provided it in his letter.

'I may say, Mrs Coulthard, that I saw many brave actions in the heat of battle, but your son's bravery extended over years; a calm, serene bravery, not only in his actions but in his spirit and character, and I count it as a great favour to have known him and shared his adventures.'

If there had indeed been any veiled resentment against Fred in that first letter, it seemed to dissipate somewhat in her second, which she sent a month later. The testaments of others who had known her son was quickly building in Dorothy Coulthard a fierce new pride in the boy she had lost; whatever tensions might once have existed between them were of no importance now.

'Every day I get a spate of letters from POWs or friends, and even people I have never heard of… and, well, he must have developed into a grand fellow.'

Blessedly for her, she was intelligent and sensitive enough to understand that Antony's years as a prisoner of the Nazis had not been the obliteration of all her hopes for him and that, in truth, the very opposite had been the case.

'Life in a POW camp gave him his life's great mission and he took it with both hands, not counting the cost, for it was with him a question of priority. What shall I put first? Where is the centre of things, the object of our striving? All his life he has always given of his best in everything he did, nothing less would satisfy him and that "giving" over five years proved too much of a strain.'

In this letter, though, a mother's grief seemed even rawer than before. The shock of the death may have worn off a little, but the reality of her loss was growing even worse.

'In time, I shall get to feel his noble spirit hovering round me and I shall dwell on the lovely things of his life and not let his tragic ending haunt me, for he didn't deserve it,' she told Fred. 'Now I understand the saying, "Those whom the Gods love die young." They give so much intensively in a short time that their course is (soon) over. But we, their mothers, are left heartbroken.'

These raw confessions must have made Fred's sadness even more acute, at the very time he was trying to deal with his own difficulties of readjustment.

Dorothy Coulthard wrote again, for the last time, six weeks later. She had been very ill, she told him; delayed shock had affected her heart, her hearing and brought on thyroid trouble. In reply, Fred mentioned the problems he, too, had been having.

'I was not at all well on my return from Germany but am now feeling more my normal self.'

Despite the polite hopes expressed on both sides that they might meet each other soon, there is no record of any such encounter. It would be understandable if Fred had quietly hoped it might never happen. But even if he never saw Dorothy Coulthard face to face, there was not the slightest possibility that he would ever forget her and that sentence she had written to him three months earlier.

In this final letter, she told him that the account he had written to her of the escape to Switzerland had been sent to the archives of The Queen's College, Oxford, her son's *alma mater*. This narrative would also form a major part of a brief memoir that some of those who knew Antony there had decided to put together as a tribute (this was published in 1946, but the author remains unknown). There was no shortage of people willing to contribute. Among them was the Reverend Lathaen, the padre at Stalag XXA.

'Letting the various memories of him pass before your eyes, you see him a true son of England... one nursed and reared in the Faith of his fathers. He was a Christian who had thought and reasoned out the Faith... and he strove to live it without talk and show. He was a humble man.'

The ultimate contributor, albeit indirectly, was King George VI. On the 23 November 1945, eight months almost to the day after Antony died, an announcement appeared in *The London Gazette*.

'The King has been graciously pleased to approve the posthumous award of a Mention-In-Despatches in recognition of gallant and distinguished service in the field to Lance Corporal J.A.R. Coulthard, Intelligence Corps.'

This citation and the medals that came with it have never been found by Antony's descendants, but it is believed the award was based on the letter sent by Fred Foster to MI9, the POWs branch of the intelligence services, describing their meticulously planned escape, their intelligence gathering in Berlin and, not least, Antony's act of gallantry in coming back to help his comrade and, in doing so, altering the course of his own life.

No doubt Fred got some comfort from this recognition of Antony, though it must have seemed small compensation for the life taken away. But when he lay in the dark at night in the tiny bedroom he had known all his life, it is more likely that he heard the anguished words of Dorothy Coulthard rather than the fine phrases of His Majesty The King.

'He made the fatal mistake of returning to help *you*.'

*

But Peggy was there to support him. Always by his side, as she would be for the next forty-five years.

In time, almost everything Fred Foster wanted from his life would come to him. The desire for children he had so often expressed in his letters from Fort 13 was soon fulfilled. A daughter, Margaret, was born in 1946 and a son Steve, the author of this book, in 1949.

Back in civvy street, armed with the professional qualifications built up in the prison camp, he had joined his cousins in their family business. This meant leaving Newark for Grantham, twelve miles away over the border into Lincolnshire. Well into his thirties now, Fred finally left the confines of 32 Bowbridge Road. With the wages the Army had continued to pay him throughout his five years' captivity, there was enough for the deposit on a small semi-detached house. He and Peggy had a home of their own at last. They were on their way.

For almost forty years he would work at Foster's Builders, rising to become its sales director. In the post-war decades, it grew steadily into one of the biggest housebuilders in the East Midlands. Fred was the brains behind the brawn, helping to guide it through recessions, strikes, the three-day week and all the other vicissitudes of post-war Britain, as the country slowly recovered from the conflict and struggled to adjust to new realities.

Yet his life was far more colourful than this suggests. In the early 1950s, he entered local politics, becoming a town councillor and then, after only four years, the youngest-ever Mayor of Grantham. For a boy who'd left school at fourteen, it was quite an achievement. Resplendent in his robes and chains of office, the bricklayer's son led his redheaded wife up the steps into Grantham's grand Victorian town hall. If only, he must have thought, his mother could have seen him. During his year in office, he was ill for a time, during which Peggy stood in for him and performed admirably. The town had never had a more appealing First Lady. As she grew older, her shyness in company abated and she blossomed considerably, becoming a councillor herself and later a Justice of the Peace.

Despite this blossoming, the marriage, however, remained a highly conventional one. That letter from Stalag XXA, asking anxiously if he was 'anything like the sort of husband she wanted' had never been necessary. Fred's intense love of his wife was reciprocated by her lifelong worship of him. He was everything to her and she was everything to him. Fred doled out the housekeeping money once a week and handled all their financial affairs (when she was widowed, Peggy had no idea how to write a cheque). He even liked to choose her new dresses, telling her in which one she looked most beautiful. Although she was a very bright woman, like many of her generation she chose to metaphorically walk one step behind her husband. Hard to understand today, but that's the way it was.

Their politics were conventional, too. Fred's character was that of the good old-fashioned 'one-nation' Tory. He had no time for socialism. As somebody who had pulled himself up by his bootstraps and made his own luck, he found it hard to understand anyone who was either unwilling or unable to do the same. Often taking his children with him, there was nothing he enjoyed more than canvassing in an election, knocking on doors and having a fiery debate with somebody who didn't agree with him.

After his time as mayor of Grantham, Fred remained a councillor and was eventually appointed an Alderman of the borough. Taking over from Alf Roberts as chairman of the school governors of the Kesteven and Grantham girls' school, he fought to keep it as a grammar school in the age of the comprehensive. When Alf's daughter, a former head girl and by now better known as Margaret Thatcher, became Prime Minister in 1979, Fred was ecstatic. He squired her around on numerous occasions when The Iron Lady visited her home town, a fact that he felt entitled him to bombard 10 Downing Street with letters soliciting her help with local issues, especially those relating to the building industry. He always received a gracious reply, though not always a concrete result.

Every year without fail, he made the trip down to London for a reunion with the boys from Stalags XXA and 383. No doubt they made jokes, most of them blue, about each other's wrinkles, paunches and double chins. Nobody told a blue joke better than Fred; the respectable ladies of Grantham might not have recognised their former Mister Mayor. They swapped stories about the bloody Jerries. Remember that bastard? Let's hope he's rotting in hell by now. As the evening wore on and things grew a little more maudlin, it is likely that glasses were raised to the boys who never made it home. In the gallery of faces that had been lost to the dark, 'The Professor' would have been one of those most fondly remembered. Unlike the middle-aged and elderly men propping up the bar, Antony would never have the wrinkles or the paunch. He would stay always young, full of promise, forever poised on the threshold of the life he was not to have.

'They shall grow not old as we that are left grow old.'

But how wonderful it would have been if he had been there on those annual evenings, no doubt a man of distinction by then, a respected diplomat, an ambassador even, but somehow still the same old 'Prof'. It is to be hoped that, on this one night of the year, the jokes, the laughter and the company of old comrades helped Fred Foster to poultice the wound of the death in the barn at Kaltenhof.

At these reunions, Sam Kydd, just as he had been in the days of Fort 13, was the life and soul of the party. He and Fred had always remained close. In the decades after the war, Sam had become an instantly recognisable face in films and on television. When he was the subject of *This Is Your Life* in 1974, Fred was one of the guests, telling Eamonn Andrews the story of how he and Sam had gone on that recce with the film unit, checking out the area around Torun before Fred and Antony's escape. But he did not mention Antony by name. Even thirty years on, it was still too difficult. And so it remained. As mentioned at the beginning of this book, Fred almost never spoke about his war, to his family at least. Sam Kydd's programme was a rare and very public exception, but even that was kept deliberately vague: just another amusing anecdote for the TV audience.

Perhaps the most extraordinary thing about the later life of Sergeant Foster is that he held little or no resentment against Germany or the Germans. One might have imagined that, like so many of those who had suffered in World War Two, he would never have wished to stand on its soil ever again. But not Fred. Down the years, he often took us on camping holidays to what had once been the Third Reich. In a little Austin A30 car, we pitched our tents all over the beauty spots of Germany and Austria.

On one of these, we went to Nuremberg, the very city where Fred and Antony, having been recaptured, had so narrowly escaped incineration on the bombed-out train. On this visit, though, Fred Foster could be the victor, not the vanquished. He stood on the very same podium where Hitler had once ranted his toxic ideology at tens of thousands of regimented acolytes. To amuse my sister and me, Fred raised his arm and gave the Nazi salute in mockery of it all and in the sweet knowledge that the Führer was now dust. He smiled as he did it, but there must have been so much sorrow behind that smile. Still, it must have been a satisfying moment. At Lake Constance that day in 1942, Adolf had got the better of him and Antony, but who had had the last laugh now?

On these holidays, Fred liked nothing more than to show off his language skills. It is unlikely that his accent ever improved. 'The Professor', up on some cloud, would still have flinched. But Fred clearly thought that, after spending all those months learning the blasted language, he was damn well going to use it. He was perfectly happy to sit outside the tent on a warm evening, having a smoke and a drink and enjoying a chat with any German who came into his orbit, many of whom had been his enemies in the war.

'None of them will admit to being bloody Nazis,' he'd whisper to us later, 'but they all were.'

When Margaret once made a holiday friendship with a German family, Fred was pretty sure that the father had been an SS man.

'You can always spot them,' he said.

And yet he did not walk away. In fact, the families became good friends and once came to stay with us in Grantham. Sergeant Foster, a prisoner of war for five long years, gave shelter beneath his roof to a man who had once been his mortal enemy. But Fred's essential nature, exactly like that of Antony Coulthard, was of a man who reached out to others. The bad times were past; never forgotten and, in many aspects, not forgiven, but let's be pals now and move on together. Since he was all too well aware by then how Antony and so many millions of others had died at the hands of the Nazis, this seems even more remarkable. But Fred knew that wars could not go on forever and that peace had to come some time. He seemed incapable of harbouring any lasting hatred or resentment towards anyone. And there was perhaps no more valuable lesson he ever taught us.

As the children of Fred and Peggy Foster, my sister Margaret and I had a warm and loving childhood. We lived in a pleasant house with a beautiful garden, where Dad built us a swing, where chickens laid the eggs we had for breakfast and where our vegetables came from our own patch, which Dad lovingly tended. Idyllic is not too strong a word.

We didn't much enjoy our dutiful trips back to Newark to visit our grandfather Harry. In contrast to our own sunny, modern home, the house at 32 Bowbridge Road seemed dark and dingy. Margaret was even too scared to go up the steep, shadowy stairs. And the old brick-layer, kind-hearted though he was, had by then developed an almost Dickensian look; his face deeply fissured from his years on the building sites, still wreathed in the smoke from his Woodbines and now totally toothless apart from one large incisor at the front, which he called his 'onion stabber'. We couldn't get out of there fast enough.

Fred was a wonderful father, but a tough one, too, when he felt the need to be. The ghost of his mother Ethel, who had drummed into him that people could achieve whatever they wanted, was never far from his shoulder. If you ran out of pocket money before the end of the week, that was just too bad. If you made a stupid mistake, you were expected to learn from it. But if you showed an aptitude for anything, if he saw that you wanted to pursue a dream, there was nothing he wouldn't do to support you.

Denied a good education himself, and having seen the value of it in a man like Antony, he was determined that his own children would study hard and make the very best of themselves, just as his old friend had done. When I went through my rebellious teenage phase, we had some bumpy times. More than once I was chased round the house and felt the flat of his hand. When I failed every single one of my 'O Levels', he was furious and frog-marched me to a technical college where eventually I earned enough passes to gain entry to a naval apprentice-ship and begin the career to which I gave my life. At every passing-out parade, Dad and Mum were always there and, in the end, I think I made him proud of me.

He was hardly less strict with my sister. If Margaret went to a dance, he would never let boys bring her home, instead collecting her himself. There was to be no smooching at his front gate. When she decided she wanted to be a doctor, he moved mountains to help her. There was none of the necessary physics teaching at her own school, so Fred made a bargain with a teacher from another school to tutor her in exchange for building him a house at a reduced price. His daughter was going to be a doctor and that was that. However, when, as a medical student, she got overdrawn at the bank, Dad refused to bail her out, forcing her to take a part-time job in a bingo hall till she'd paid it off. Having started life poor, he understood the transformative power of money and wanted his children to appreciate it, too. But when Margaret eventually graduated, he was thrilled to bits.

'Didn't I do well with Margaret?' he said to her, as if it had been his achievement rather than hers, which of course, in one sense, it was.

As I've already emphasised, despite those German holidays and his trips to London for the POW reunions, Dad almost never mentioned his own direct experiences of war. He certainly didn't talk about Antony Coulthard, though now of course I understand why.

Once, only once, did he let a chink of light shine in on that friendship that had meant so much to him so long ago. In Fred's last years, he and Peggy left Grantham and moved to a village in Dorset within easy reach of where both Margaret and I and their grandchildren were now living: Margaret as a general practitioner and me as an Engineer Officer in the Royal Navy.

By pure coincidence, Margaret's son became a pupil at King Edward VI School in Southampton, where Antony had been half a century before. When Fred casually glanced at the programme for a school prize-giving, he came across the name of Antony Coulthard, after whom a prize for modern languages was now given. Fred circled the name with a pen, but otherwise said nothing. But the circling in the programme was later noticed and questions were asked. Oh, just a chap he knew in the war, he said. That was all. He was then told that the name was emblazoned on the panelled walls of the school. His grandson asked if Fred would like to go and see it. He replied that he would. And one day the two of them did just that. Yet still he confided little to his family about this chap from the war. He did not show them how his heart felt. The day came and went. Nothing more was said.

It seems pretty clear to me now that, after the death of Antony Coulthard, Fred Foster lived for the rest of his days with what we now call 'survivor's guilt'. He had had a fine life: a loving wife who had been the blessing of his existence and two children whom he had nurtured and to whom he had given everything of himself. He had achieved many things and made his mark on the world. Everyone knew and liked Fred Foster, a man without enemies. In short, he had enjoyed all those precious things that Antony never had the chance to experience. All the hopes and dreams 'The Professor' had cherished had died with him on the earthen floor of a barn in Kaltenhof.

And perhaps, of course, they needn't have. If, on that sunny August day at Lake Constance, with the mountains of Switzerland and freedom right there on the horizon, Antony had not come back for him. But he had, instinctively and without a second thought, despite the agreement they had made beforehand. Because that, quite simply, was the man Antony was. But it was hard for Fred to be the beneficiary of that act of gallantry. An act he had in no way sought and would undoubtedly have tried to prevent had that been feasible. But that was what had happened and he was powerless to change it.

Fred never really settled in Dorset. His professional life had come to an unfortunate conclusion when, on the very verge of his retirement, Foster's Builders went into decline and, ultimately, liquidation, owing considerable debts. He had seen this coming and done his best to prevent it, but his counsel wasn't listened to by some of his relatives in the family business. As a prominent figure in Grantham for over thirty years, Fred felt the humiliation of it keenly and it was a large part of why he and Peggy headed south.

But Dad's roots in the East Midlands were too tenacious to be successfully transplanted elsewhere. In his final years, he became more withdrawn, turning in on himself, losing something of his good cheer and his lifelong resilience to the slings and arrows of fortune. So, as a means of raising his spirits, we all looked forward to 24 February 1990. The Golden Wedding Anniversary of Fred and Peggy Foster. A huge party was planned. People were coming from all over, especially from up north. But Fred had been getting niggling pains for a while and these became rapidly worse. A kidney problem was diagnosed; it would have to be removed. It was hardly a minor operation but they promised he would recover in time for the party.

But the procedure was botched. The kidney was removed, but one of his major arteries was not sealed correctly and he suffered a massive internal bleed, which in turn triggered a minor stroke. It was decided to move him to a hospital with greater facilities. There was an ambulance strike that week and an army ambulance appeared, crewed by a team of soldiers. Desperately ill though he was, Dad was delighted; eager to know to which regiments they belonged, what rank they bore and where they had served. He'd been in the Sherwood Foresters, he told them. Got captured in Norway. Was a guest of Adolf for five long years. At the sight of uniforms, the 'old' Fred seemed to have re-emerged for a moment. But it was just one last flare of the candle. A day later, he suffered a second, massive stroke. At the age of seventy-five, Dad died just three weeks before he and Mum would have toasted their fifty-year love affair. In the end, one little kidney did what Hitler and the Third Reich had singularly failed to achieve, and finished off Sergeant Fred Foster.

The guests who had been invited to the party instead turned up for the funeral. The Royal British Legion did him proud and, with their medals shining in the winter sun, many of the POWs from both Stalag XXA and Stalag 383 came to the little church in Dorset to salute their old comrade for the last time. Their numbers now were naturally fewer. His great pal Sam Kydd had gone eight years earlier, much too young at only sixty-seven. For many of them, old age and illness made journeys harder, but there was still a pretty good 'show' for Fred Foster. At the wake, the old stories and jokes I'd heard before swirled around my head, but I didn't take much of it in. Like my mother and sister, I walked around in a sort of daze. As the old men drifted off towards their taxis and their trains, I knew it was unlikely I would ever see any of them again. I imagined that their place in my consciousness would melt away with the death of my father. But I was to be quite wrong about that.

On 24 February, the day of their anniversary, Mum somehow dressed herself up. My sister and I took her out to lunch. But it was a fruitless exercise. There was an empty place at the table, a ghost at the feast and, without him, we had no stomach for it. Still numb with shock and sadness, the three of us sat almost silently, staring at our plates.

Heartbroken and totally bereft, Peggy struggled to carry on alone. But the centre of her universe had gone and life no longer seemed to have much point for her. By one of those bizarre coincidences, I too became seriously ill with kidney problems, possibly due to severe dehydration, while serving in the Persian Gulf. After a similarly messed-up operation to that of my father, I too came close to death. Naturally, my mother was distraught at the possibility her only son might perish in precisely the same circumstances as her husband had done only months before. I eventually pulled through, but the strain of it further weakened Mum's diminishing appreciation of being alive. Cancer soon claimed her, which my sister felt certain was triggered by stress and loss. Less than two years after Dad passed away, Mum quietly followed. As she always had in life, the pretty redhead from Barnard Castle walked one step behind him into death. It was impossible not to feel it was a mercy.

Not long before, she had reminded us about Fred's old suitcase from the war.

'There are some tales in there,' she'd said.

CHAPTER THIRTEEN

I realised at once that I had to do it. As soon as I devoured the contents of my father's old suitcase that day in 2010, there hadn't been the shadow of a doubt. Sixty-five years on from the events described in it, the whole story was not yet told. Its last words were not yet written and never could be till one big question was answered. Where was the body of Antony Coulthard?

His parents and, much later, both his sisters had all gone to their own graves still not knowing where their son and brother himself lay at rest. That had always been a bitter extra blow for a family dealing with bereavement. The only commemoration of his death was the inclusion of his name on Column 155 of the Commonwealth War Graves Commission monument at Dunkirk. Since Antony had not taken part in that historic retreat, it must have seemed the feeblest of memorials. Hardly somewhere they might want to go to cry and lay flowers.

But he had remained a constant presence in the minds of his family and the cherished memory of him was handed down to the new generation, the children of his sisters. The short, dramatic life of Uncle Antony was a cause of sadness to be sure, but also a source of immense pride. Pride that they shared the blood of such a remarkable man. The memoir of her son that Dorothy had commissioned just after his death was known to them all. Everyone was familiar with what happened at Lake Constance, when Antony had turned back for Fred. I wondered what they all felt about that. By now of course the suitcase had convinced me that my father had felt responsible, albeit indirectly, for his friend's death. Did his descendants share that belief?

On an intellectual level, it was perfectly possible to refute any 'guilt' at all. If Antony had *not* turned back, or if either or both of them had made it into Switzerland then home to Britain, what would then have happened? The certainty is that, after a period of recuperation, they would have been called back into military service. Antony, with his linguistic skills, could well have been put into the Special Operations Executive and parachuted right back into Germany. Fred would have returned to the Sherwood Foresters, battalions of which took part in post D-Day operations in northwest Europe and were embroiled in the vicious fighting in Italy. So the probability, and a strong one, too, is that either or both of them might have been killed, or at least recaptured, long before the champagne corks popped on VE Day.

So it was illogical for me to believe that my father had caused the ultimate death of his friend. But 'guilt' on an emotional, visceral level was a different thing entirely. By now I was quite sure *that* was the kind of guilt Fred Foster had lived with for the remaining forty-five years of his life. A guilt immune to reasoning or argument. And now, as his son, I knew it had wormed its way inside me, too. An act of heroism had occurred on the shores of Lake Constance and I felt that my family did indeed owe a debt to Antony's. So what greater reparation could I possibly make than to find his grave and, in a sense, give him back to them? But not only did I have no idea where Antony was, I didn't know the whereabouts of his descendants either. I made up my mind to find both.

The search would be hard, tiring, frustrating, maddening. I would get lost among the dusty shelves of libraries and along fruitless routes of enquiry. I would have sore feet, sore eyes and, very often, a sore heart when I began to think the whole thing was impossible and that I should have to admit defeat. But the longer I searched for Antony, the more compulsive it became. I knew that I would not, *could* not, rest till I had found him.

I started out by writing to any authority that might conceivably have some knowledge of the circumstances of his death: King Edward VI School in Southampton, the Commonwealth War Graves Commission (CWGC), the Ministry of Defence section who held his service records and that which dealt with veterans. I wrote to the pastor of the church at Dömitz where Antony's mother had originally told my father that her son had been buried. I wrote to the pastors of churches in the surrounding countryside. Everyone was polite and helpful but not one could further my quest for Antony. At every turn, it was brick walls and dead ends.

I then began a period of many months' travelling on my beloved motorbike between my home near Winchester and the Intelligence Corps headquarters, the National Archives at Kew and the Imperial War Museum. I spent long days going through old documents looking for any evidence of the circumstances of Antony's death. Time after time, I got home, tired and dispirited, the expression on my face telling my wife that, yet again, I had found nothing much.

Then the gods decided to smile down on me. One day in the National Archives, I had started to feel my quest was hopeless. I had almost decided that the next file the attendant would slap down on the table in front of me would be the last. I opened it wearily and began to scan the pages. I sat bolt upright. By God, this was it. This was the affidavit written to the War Crimes Commission by Staff Sergeant Aitken, that feisty NCO from Antony's column on the Forced March. Here was the harrowing testimony of the conditions on the Forced March. Written almost seventy years before, the anger in Thomas Aitken's words bounced off the page as if he had written them yesterday.

In particular, his vitriol was directed at the cruelty of Hauptmann Mackensen and his vicious guards. I soon discovered that it had been this damning evidence of Aitken's that had led to Mackensen being tried for the murder of thirty British soldiers who had died on the march. So damning was it that, when Aitken stood up to testify at the trial, he was only part of the way through his evidence when Mackensen realised his defence was hopeless and changed his plea to guilty. The Commission agreed with his own verdict on himself, and had hanged him in 1946. Whatever one's views on capital punishment, it was very hard to find pity for the man who, if he'd had a little more of the milk of human kindness in his veins, might have treated Antony and the other sick prisoners with more compassion and possibly saved their lives. As things stood, he was, in my eyes, Antony's true murderer. The list of those thirty soldiers was also in the file. Lance Corporal Antony Coulthard was the last name on the list in the last file I had intended to open before throwing in the towel. Eureka.

Now the gods decided to bless me again. For months, I had been joining websites about World War Two, posting Antony's name and the story of his and my father's escape from Stalag XXA. The online thread became busier; more and more people were wanting to know all about Antony and Fred. Out of the blue, to my amazement, I was contacted by a woman called Barbara Willoughby-Thomas from Australia. This was Antony's niece, the daughter of his younger sister Pamela, and she, too, had started an attempt to find her uncle's grave. How extraordinary that sixty-five years after his death, two people, strangers to each other, were on the same mission at the very same time. But we were strangers no longer. From now on, Barbara and I were to become staunch allies in the search. Someone who had an even greater emotional stake in it than I did. It was too good to be true.

Suddenly, all those brick walls seemed to crumble and the dead ends began to lead somewhere. The historian of the Intelligence Corps, the late Major Alan Edwards, invited me to his office and threw open all of the Corps' records. Once again, in a room crammed with regiments of ancient files, I pulled up a chair, began to dig and was rewarded almost at once. I found a letter sent in June 1945 by the POW Casualty Directorate to Antony's father confirming that his son had not been buried in the churchyard at Dömitz at all, but in Kaltenhof, the site of the barn where he had died. This information had never been passed on by Antony's mother in her sequence of letters to my father that summer; an understandable omission by a grieving woman still in a state of shock. Or perhaps she felt the detail hardly mattered.

Barbara Willoughby-Thomas then contacted her cousin in England, Andrew Robinson, the son of Antony's older sister Daphne and now a distinguished author. Did he have any material relating to their uncle's death? He had two.

The first was a copy of a letter that had landed on the Coulthards' doormat in 1947. This was from Private Dennis Bonner who claimed to have been with Antony in the barn when he died. Among other things, this letter reconfirmed that the grave was not in Dömitz. But Bonner's letter also included a sketch map of the area, which revealed that it was not in Kaltenhof *either*, for the simple reason that the hamlet had no cemetery. The grave, said Bonner, must be in a village some distance to the south, because this was the direction in which the Forced March had continued on the day of Antony's death. This could only be Quickborn, the only place in the immediate locality with a burial ground.

The second document Andrew Robinson sent was a handwritten sketch map of the countryside on the west bank of the River Elbe. At some point in this immediate post-war period, the Coulthards had asked two friends, who were allowed into Germany as part of the Inter Allied Commission, to try to investigate Private Bonner's testimony. When these friends eventually reported back, they enclosed this sketch map. The notes scribbled on it were in German, which possibly meant it had been drawn by local people approached to help. This map, plus Bonner's evidence, reconfirmed that Quickborn was indeed 'The Professor's' final destination. The Coulthards had then sent this evidence to the Directorate of Graves' Registration and Enquiries, who had promised to forward it on to their searcher teams in Germany.

The question now entered my mind as to why the Coulthards or their other children had never gone to Germany to try to find Antony's grave. Surely the path Barbara and I were now trying to follow could also have been followed by them, sixty-five years earlier, albeit with considerably more difficulty in the pre-internet age. Nevertheless, it is quite conceivable that they would have eventually found him, hopefully giving themselves a bit of what we now call 'closure'. They would surely have passed on the information to Fred Foster and given him that same comfort. So why didn't they?

At the end of the war, Europe was bruised, battered and bloodied. As its map was being redrawn, chaos and confusion reigned everywhere, especially in the defeated Third Reich. Travel was restricted to all but the most necessary military and civilian personnel. Those Thomas Cook brochures of cheery blonde girls in *dirndls* holding tall glasses of frothing beer had not yet reappeared. More pertinently, the victors had been busy dividing the spoils and The Iron Curtain soon came down with a swift and fearsome crash. In northwest Germany, its frontier was designated as the River Elbe.

This is an important fact in our story. It meant that the small town of Dömitz was now in the Soviet-occupied Eastern Zone, but the barn at Kaltenhof where Antony died and the cemetery at Quickborn, though only a mile or so away on the opposite bank, were in the Western Allied Zone (later called West Germany). It seems possible that, due to a combination of raw grief and political uncertainty, the Coulthards were unable to grasp the significance of the various documents that were sent to them and went on believing that Antony's resting place was in Soviet territory and completely inaccessible. Perhaps nobody had yet produced newly detailed maps of the re-drawn Germany. Perhaps nobody told the Coulthards, either then or later, that they might go and lay flowers on their boy's grave. Or maybe they now hated Germany so much that they simply refused to set foot in it.

In the immediate aftermath of war, the task facing the Allied searcher teams had been staggering. A whole year after the end of hostilities, more than one hundred and fifty thousand graves had still to be located, of which thirty-three thousand would turn out to be those of 'unknown soldiers'. In 2010, when Antony's niece and I joined forces, we did not know that he had become one of these 'unknowns'. Our expectation had been that, in the little churchyard at Quickborn, his grave was lying there just waiting for us to find him. It wasn't going to be that simple.

On the morning of 24 March 1945, as his four comrades had buried him at Quickborn, the column was already marching south. The vile Mackensen had ordered that the interment should be done quickly so that the march would not be held up. As his friends buried Antony, the German soldiers were breathing right down their necks. This had forced them to hurriedly ask a civilian to erect a wooden cross above the grave with Antony's name, rank and date of death. But either this cross had subsequently been removed or lost – or had never been put there in the first place.

The second, even more important fact which, in 2010, Barbara and I did not know, was that the overworked searcher teams had, in fact, found the body of Antony Coulthard *but without knowing who he was*. In 1947, in the cemetery at Quickborn, they had come across the graves of two *unidentified* British soldiers. It was decided that these two anonymous bodies would be moved to rest among their fellows at the new war cemetery at Becklingen, about fifty miles to the west near Soltau in Lower Saxony.

But *why* was Antony's grave unidentified? Was the 'villain of the piece' the unknown German civilian whom the burial party had been forced to ask to mark the grave at Quickborn with his name, rank and number? Had some trivial incident prevented the man from doing so? Had his wife suddenly called him to come in for breakfast? Did he have a lousy headache or an aching back? Had he stuffed a scrap of paper with Antony's details, hastily scribbled by the burial party, into a pocket and forgotten all about it? Or had he lost the piece of paper? Did he therefore just erect a simple wooden cross without identification? Or maybe he'd just thought to hell with the whole thing and never bothered to do even that? It was the grave of an enemy after all. We cannot know the truth, but we know the outcome. That the location of the remains of Antony Coulthard now became 'lost' for the next sixty-five years.

Still believing him to be at rest in Quickborn, I wrote to the Commonwealth War Graves Commission asking if they had any knowledge of Lance Corporal Coulthard's grave. They replied that they had no specific knowledge of him, but that two 'unknown'

British soldiers had been removed from Quickborn in July 1947 and reinterred in Becklingen war cemetery. They even provided the precise location of these two soldiers. Plot 18, Row C, Graves 1&2. Was it possible Antony was one of these two soldiers? We simply didn't know.

In 2012, Antony's niece and I decided the time had come for us to travel to Germany. Barbara and her son Tom flew halfway across the world from their home in Australia, while I had the far easier journey from the UK, which I made on my beloved motorcycle. We had been advised by the Commonwealth War Graves Commission that we had to find indisputable, linking documentary evidence from the place of death to one of these two graves at Becklingen cemetery if it was to be recognised as that of Antony Coulthard. Only written evidence would be admissible. Exhumation for DNA testing with possible next-of-kin would not be allowed.

So it was down to us. On 21 May 2012, the son of Fred Foster and the niece and great-nephew of Antony Coulthard met at the hamlet of Kaltenhof where Antony had died sixty-seven years before. We saw the pretty town of Dömitz on the opposite bank of the Elbe. We saw the ruins of the old railway bridge that he would have seen, the same flat fields, the same trees. The last, hazy landscape of his life, before his body shut down and he could see no more. And then, most difficult of all, we saw the barn itself, miraculously still standing after all this time.

Here we were met by two local historians who had kindly agreed to show us around the village. I had found these men through the German Tourist Board and, prior to our meeting, one had placed an article in a local newspaper detailing our search for the grave and asking if any readers in the locality might be able to help us. We hadn't had high expectations of this article, but we got far more than we'd bargained for.

An elderly man had responded. His name was Hermann Apitz. Back in 1945, when he was thirteen years old, the barn had been part of his father's farm. He agreed to meet us there and tell us what he knew. With the local historians acting as interpreters, Herr Apitz told us how he clearly remembered the day that the exhausted column of two hundred or so prisoners had trudged up the lane. But he recalled more than that. On the morning of 24 March, he had been playing in the farmyard when some British soldiers had shouted to him in German that one of their comrades had died in the night and that he should run and find the guards. The old Hermann Apitz still remembered seeing Antony's body, covered with a tarpaulin, now lying near the door of the barn. It was a strange feeling to be looking into the same eyes that had witnessed that sight almost seventy years before. He then led us to the exact spot where the body had rested. It was a profoundly emotional moment for us all, but especially upsetting for Barbara and her son Tom. Again, that visceral 'guilt' I felt rose up in me. If only Antony hadn't turned back to help Fred Foster.

Hermann Apitz was certain that Antony had been buried down the road at Quickborn and that a second British POW, part of a later column, who had also died in the barn a few weeks after Antony, had been laid there too. We asked him to sign a piece of paper testifying to that, which he willingly did. We all shook hands and wished each other well. I found myself hoping he'd had a happy life, after the sad things he'd had to witness as a child.

We hurried the short distance to the church at Quickborn, where we were met by the pastor. He confirmed again that two British soldiers had been buried in the cemetery there just before the end of the war. Unfortunately, all the records from that period had been lost due to severe fighting between the German and American armies in the area. However, a very elderly retired gravedigger could still remember the position of the graves before their removal by the searcher teams in 1947 and had now given a statement to that effect. The pastor also showed us a wooden cross that had been placed above *one* of the graves and had been kept by the church when the bodies were taken away. Sadly, the cross carried no name, nor was there evidence of any second such cross. But because no fighting had ever taken place in that area between German and *British* forces, these two graves could only have been dug for dead British servicemen on POW columns passing through. So we now had two pieces of signed documentary evidence from living witnesses that one of the two bodies taken from the old graveyard at Quickborn had to be that of Antony Coulthard.

Barbara, Tom and I then went westwards to Becklingen. This was not a town or a village, just a large open space cleared out of the thickly wooded countryside. It was a beautiful place, the breeze rustling gently through the tall trees that surrounded the burial-ground like sentinels. We walked among the endless rows of plain, white marble headstones, looking for the numbers we had been given by the CWGC. The three of us were both nervous and emotional. At this point, we expected that we would find the graves of two unknown soldiers and would never learn in which of the two Antony rested. And that was going to be hard. Better than nothing of course, far better. At least the family would know roughly where he lay, and that was a splendid thing. But it would not allow us to reclaim him in the way we wanted to do, by giving him back his name, chiselling it into the hard marble so that he would never lose it again.

The two headstones came into focus. We checked the numbers once more. Plot 18, Row C, Graves 1&2. They were the ones alright. And then a little miracle occurred. These were not the graves of *two* uniden-tified soldiers. To our complete surprise, Grave 1 was clearly marked with a name, rank and number: that of Bombardier Kershaw of the Duke of Wellington's Regiment. Somehow, in years gone by, other people like us must have trodden the same path and had managed to prove that their loved one was the occupant of Grave 1. This meant only one thing. That the neighbouring plot, Grave 2, the resting place of 'a soldier of the 1939-45' war, was that of Antony Coulthard. It was an extraordinary moment. We had found him.

It is strange how one can be exhilarated and deeply sad at the same time. How smiles and tears can be on your face simultaneously. For nearly seven decades, Antony had lain here in this corner of a foreign field, far away from home. Now the child of his sister, someone of his own flesh and blood, was standing beside him. His family had come to claim him.

*

It is hard to overstate the joy that we felt that afternoon in 2012. But our trip to Europe was not yet finished. Now happy that we finally knew where Antony lay in death, we wanted to see for ourselves the place where he had perhaps come most alive. The place where, as Dorothy Coulthard had written to Fred Foster, 'life had given him his great mission'. Stalag XXA in Poland.

Barbara and Tom took their own route east, while I got back on my motorcycle. I had decided to follow the route of Antony's column in reverse. It took me only two days' riding in the glorious late-spring sunshine through beautiful wooded countryside, camping out each night, to reach Torun. Seventy years earlier, it had taken the hungry, sick and freezing prisoners eight weeks to cover the same distance in the grim grip of winter.

At Torun I reunited with Barbara and Tom, and we were now joined by my sister Margaret and her son Christopher. How astonished Antony and Fred would have been that their descendants were walking through the gates of Fort 13 and across the drawbridge into the prison that had confined them for five long years. I could almost hear Dad's voice in my head.

'What did you want to go back *there* for? Miserable bloody place.'

The old Prussian forts of Torun, once Stalag XXA, were still mostly intact and now open to the public; part museum, part tourist attraction. We went inside the dank chambers where the unlikely friendship between Antony and Fred had blossomed, where they had spent long evenings teaching Fred German and plotting their great escape. The peeling, whitewashed walls were still covered in the prisoners' graffiti, which showed, despite the harsh conditions in which they were forced to live, the level of defiance shown by the POWs to their German captors. Private Hughes of The Worcesters got five days for not saluting a German officer and, the graffiti says 'he'll do five more before he ever salutes the bastard'. We saw where the 'Little Theatre' had once been, where Sam Kydd had put on his variety shows and where boys had dressed as girls in *Charley's Aunt*. We saw, too, the bricked-up entrance to the 'cooler', where Antony and Fred would have done their time after being recaptured at Lake Constance.

Gradually, we recognised places that had appeared in the old photographs found in Dad's suitcase, especially the grassy bank where Antony and Fred had posed for their pictures just days before they had made their escape. It was extraordinary to have our own photos taken standing in the exact same spot, seventy years on.

Before we left Fort 13, we made one final bow to Fred and 'The Professor', by following the route of their escape from the camp. Amazingly, many of the buildings still existed. The Stalag HQ, where Dad had edited the camp newspaper and where the letters from 32 Bowbridge Road and the Villa Vita had arrived in the censor's office for scrutiny. The house outside of which the German sergeant and his wife had dozed in their deck chairs. The dormitory from whose windows the German soldiers had leaned out to flirt with the Polish girls. The stable block, out of which Antony and Fred had once leapt to the ground in their new suits and trilby hats, was long gone, but the path out to the main road was still there. The path along which they had once walked with their hearts in their mouths, expecting at any second to feel a Nazi bullet in their backs. But it had been their path to freedom and they had both possessed the guts to take it. Barbara and Tom, Margaret, Christopher and I all felt pretty proud that we could claim two such men as our own.

But what might have seemed to be the end of a road was, in one sense, just the beginning. We had found Antony. The man who lay in the earth of Plot 18, Row C, Grave 2 at Becklingen was no longer 'unknown', at least not as far as the Coulthards and Fosters were concerned. But the long search for Antony was followed by an equally lengthy struggle to give him back his name. To have the grave officially recognised would take us another three whole years.

One understands the need for certainty in such important matters; there must be no rush to judgement. But Barbara and I never imagined how slow the process would be. On our return from Europe, we had immediately forwarded the fresh evidence we had gathered to the Commonwealth War Graves Commission. But there always seemed to be yet more paperwork to be filled in, yet more proof required. Week after week, month after month, the letters and emails flew to and fro between Barbara and me and the Commonwealth War Graves Commission, and the Joint Casualty and Compassionate Centre (JCCC) of The Ministry of Defence. It felt like an endless process.

A major part of the problem was that we were far from being the only people still trying to track down the last resting places of soldiers lost in both World Wars. There was a serious backlog and limited resources. Despite lobbying at the highest level by The Intelligence Corps, the National POW Association and even by myself as a retired naval commander, we just had to, quite rightly, take our place in the queue.

Luckily, The Intelligence Corps had been on our side from the beginning. In 2013, they pulled out all the stops, hosting an Antony Coulthard Day at their headquarters at Chicksands, Bedfordshire. A classroom was to be named after him. By now, I had put together a lecture, illustrated with photographs and maps, about the story of Antony and Fred's escape from Stalag XXA. I delivered it to a full house of soldiers and also to Antony's nephew Andrew Robinson, who had been so helpful in our search, his sister Natasha and cousin Cecilia, and several more Coulthards and Fosters. Much of the story none of them had heard before.

But it would not be until 24 March 2015, seventy years to the very day on which Antony had perished, that I received an email from the highly proactive JCCC case officer, Nicola Nash. It stated that The Ministry of Defence now agreed with the findings presented to it. Plot 18, Row C, Grave 2 at Becklingen would be recognised as the resting place of Antony Coulthard. It was better than winning the Lottery.

Events then began to move very fast indeed. As the saying goes, we had waited three years for a bus to come along, then several came at once. On the 18 July, my wife Christine and I were invited back to the headquarters of the Intelligence Corps to be presented with an award by their Colonel-in-Chief. For once I hadn't done my research properly, and was surprised to discover that this was the Duke of Edinburgh himself. I was also made an honorary life member of the Intelligence Corps Association. On the very same day an article about the story appeared in the *Daily Telegraph*.

But the most important day was still to come. The day that capped everything. One of the most memorable of my life.

*

I took three steps forward from the lines of mourners and stood alone in front of the grave. It had been a long, difficult journey to reach this place. Nearly five years. As long as the war itself. I had put on my old uniform and polished up my medals. It somehow mattered to me that I should be here as a military man and not as a civilian. This was a soldier's funeral after all. I tried to stand as straight-backed as I used to do on the parade ground. I raised my fingertips to my temple. Wordlessly, I thanked him and wished him peace. As a naval officer, I had saluted hundreds, perhaps thousands, of men and women, but I had never saluted anyone who deserved it more.

On the 15 July 2015, the 'unknown' grave at Becklingen was rededicated. The Commonwealth War Graves Commission had crafted a handsome new headstone with the details of Antony's name, rank and number, the date of his death and the insignia of the Intelligence Corps. The family had written a special inscription.

'A man of character, cheerfulness and nobility of spirit. Loved and admired. So many owe him so much.'

Still an obsessional motorcyclist, addicted to the lure of the open road, I had decided that I would bike all the way to Germany. Riding alone, the miles stretching endlessly ahead, is always exhilarating. It gives you time to think, too. On the journey to Becklingen, my mind had been filled with thoughts of Antony and of my father Fred. How brave they had both been in the face of adversity in Stalag XXA. Even braver at the point of Gestapo pistols that day at Lake Constance. Neither had been a professional soldier: they were just a language student and a solicitor's clerk. How scared they must have felt, yet how defiant they still managed to be. As I had often done throughout the process of uncovering the story, I wondered if I would have shown these same qualities.

The Coulthard and the Foster families, along with representatives of the Ministry of Defence and the Intelligence Corps, were to gather at a hotel in a village close to the cemetery. But before going there, I had ridden alone to look at the newly created grave. For some reason, I'd had the need to spend a few minutes with Antony by myself. The search that Barbara and I had made for him had probably been the most satisfying achievement of my life. I can hardly describe my feelings standing beside his proud new headstone on that summer afternoon. I wrote before that I'd hoped I could, in a way, give him back to those who loved him most. And now I felt that I'd managed to do that. The debt which, for the last seventy years, my family had owed to his had now been repaid.

That evening in the hotel, I'd worked hard at introducing strangers and drawing everyone together. For the second time, Barbara had flown halfway across the world, bringing her husband Glenn and son Tom. Her cousin Natasha had come from the UK, as had my daughter Celeste and my sister Margaret's son Christopher. As such things often do, it had begun a little stiffly but, after a few drinks, everyone had relaxed and all went well. It was good to see the descendants of Coulthard and Foster enjoying each other's company. Who would ever have imagined that might happen one day? Certainly not Antony and Fred.

In consultation with Barbara and me, Nicola Nash of the JCCC and the Intelligence Corps had organised the whole event, planning everything down to the finest detail. Antony had been one of the Corps' own and they were determined to do their best for him and his family. On the morning of 30 July, we were joined by a uniformed platoon from the Intelligence Corps based in Germany, many of whom were Lance Corporals, as Antony had been. In the hotel, I gave everyone a talk about the story of Antony and Fred and the 'glorious failure' of 1942.

At the gates of Becklingen cemetery, we were met by the Regimental Sergeant Major and the Padre. Here, Nicola Nash gave us wreaths to which we could attach our personal messages. To my surprise, I found this simple thing very hard to do and struggled to compose myself.

'With respect and grateful thanks from the family of your friend, Sergeant Fred Foster.'

The RSM and the Padre led us in a single line towards Plot 18, Row C, Grave 2, the Coulthards in front, the Fosters following behind. I walked beside my daughter, who had never before seen me in my best uniform. She whispered how proud she was that day, which nearly set me off again, but we somehow made it to the graveside.

I needn't have worried about anything. The Padre, Clive Larret, was magnificent, delivering a simple, moving service, which celebrated Antony as both a soldier and a man. Some others spoke, too, but, shamefully, I found myself only half-listening to their tributes. Images crowded into my mind's eye: Antony and Fred leaping from the stable loft, the emaciated Antony dying in the barn, my father reading Dorothy Coulthard's letter for the first time and the awful shock of it.

The wreaths were laid around the grave; the green and red blazing out against the cool white headstone, garlands for a hero. It will sound odd, a bit high-flown perhaps, but when it was my turn to place my wreath, I somehow saw the person standing there not as myself but as the spirit of my father. It was Fred saluting Antony.

It had fallen to me to read Robert Burns's *Epitaph on a Friend*.

> *An honest man here lies at rest*
> *As e'er God with his image blest*
> *The friend of man, the friend of truth*
> *The friend of age and guide of youth*
> *Few hearts like his with virtue warmed*
> *Few heads with knowledge so informed*
> *If there's another world, he lives in bliss*
> *If there is none, he made the best of this.*

As they listened, people linked arms and tears were shed.

The platoon's bugler sounded *The Last Post*, followed by two minutes' poignant silence. Those in uniform saluted, those not simply bowed their heads in tribute to 'The Professor'. Then he raised the bugle again to play *The Reveille* signifying that, while we must honour our dead, life goes on. By now, emotions were running high, not least when a small group of us was asked to lay hands on the headstone whilst it was blessed. The Padre had judged things perfectly by inviting a young female Lance Corporal, about the same age as Antony had been, to touch the stone along with the family and Colonel Murray ADC, Colonel of the Intelligence Corps. It was clear to see that all the young soldiers felt privileged to be part of the ceremony. Antony's comrades in the 21st century did him proud.

Once the service was over, a palpable change of mood came over those gathered together on that summer day. Sadness and grief were replaced by joy and celebration. After all, something rather wonderful had just happened. People felt free to smile and talk, wandering among rows of other headstones, looking at the names of others who had never made it home.

We left Antony to rest in this gentle woodland in the heart of the Germany he had once so loved and which, despite everything, he had probably gone on loving right till the end. He had always known that Germany and Nazism were not synonymous, that the Nazis were a virus that had run rampant for a time but which, in the end, would be eradicated. And so it would prove. Instead of being a disgrace to Europe, Germany is now an example. The country of Goethe, Schiller and Beethoven has been reborn. How proud that would have made 'The Professor'. He would surely have been well content to lie forever in that new Germany. On one side of him was Bombardier Kershaw of The Duke of Wellington's Regiment who had also perished in the barn at Kaltenhof; on the other, Corporal Frost of The Green Howards. Like Antony, both in their twenties, both dying in the final days of the war. Like him, they hadn't quite made it.

Chapter Thirteen

If only that memorable day at Becklingen had somehow happened many years earlier, so that Dorothy and John Coulthard and their daughters could have stood here and found some solace in this beautiful place.

And what about Fred Foster? The soldier who *had* made it, who had enjoyed the long life that the young men of Becklingen had lost. What might he have felt about the events of that July afternoon? In 2015, had he lived, Fred would have just turned one hundred years old. How wonderful if he had been there with us that day, standing beside me, saluting his old friend; silently thanking 'The Professor' for his comradeship, his wit and wisdom, his bravery and daring. And for coming back for him, seventy summers before. How pleased he would have been that the two families now knew each other and had come together beside Antony's grave. If only he could have witnessed 'The Professor', no longer an unknown soldier, being ceremoniously laid to rest with his kith and kin around him, it might have given Fred some of the same comfort that I hoped the Coulthards had now found.

The sad truth is that, had Dad not hidden the guilt he felt inside a dusty suitcase, all that might have happened. Had he instead shared it with his children, he and I might even have searched for Antony together. The memorable day at Becklingen might have taken place decades before. And the relationship I had with him might have been infinitely richer than it was.

Inside that suitcase, I had discovered not just an exciting and moving tale about World War Two. I also found out that I had never really known my father. Now though, I felt that I did. And that, I suppose, was my real reward.

POSTSCRIPT

1986. King Edward VI School, Southampton.

An old man and a boy stand in the great hall of an ancient school. They look up at the high walls, panelled in rich, dark wood. The panels are populated by the gilded names of those who have, down the long years, distinguished themselves in one way or another. Those who have won medals or prizes, by virtue of either brains or brawn. The geniuses at Latin or Greek. The captains of cricket or rugby.

On some of the panels, the wood is still young, the golden names blazing out sharp and clear. On others though, the wood is deeply fissured, the gilding cracked and flaky, the names faded in the long years since they were first emblazoned there. This is the list of the fallen, the young lives lost to war. It is to one of these panels that the boy leads the old man and points up to a name.

'There he is, grandfather.'

'Ah right. There he is.'

The old man looks up at it, but says nothing more. He offers no tales, sheds no tears. That is not his way. He is over seventy now: a little stooped, no longer the figure of his prime. He has been lucky to reach his biblical three-score years and ten; he knows that only too well. But he has done so and he is proud of the life he has achieved. It is a life that began with no great expectations but, by hard work and determination, he has made himself into a man of substance. A man admired by everyone who knows him, his name respected even by those who do not.

He has been blessed in so many ways. For almost half a century, his days have been illuminated by a great, enduring love. He has raised two fine children who have fulfilled his dreams for them. And now his grandchildren are nearly grown and ready to fly.

How odd it is, he thinks, that the tangled web of coincidence and circumstance should one day bring him here. But such is the way of it. Wheels within wheels. Life coming full circle. He needs no panelled wall to remind him of the name he stares at now. For over forty years, it has never been far from his thoughts.

For a while, the old man and the boy stand there silently. The boy imagines that his grandfather bears himself a little straighter than he did just a minute ago. The boy waits to be told a story, to be given entry to a memory, but soon realises it is not going to happen. The old man gives a soft sigh and walks away, back out into the daylight. The visit is not spoken of again.

AUTHOR'S NOTE

As this book relates, the very brave Sergeant Thomas Aitken testified to The War Crimes Commission that thirty men had died on Antony Coulthard's column on the Forced March in early 1945. Of those thirty men, seven were listed as having unknown graves. In the wake of finding and rededicating Antony's grave in the Becklingen War Cemetery, and having learnt a lot about the procedures and complexities of these things, I decided that I would put it to good use and try to find the remaining six. It did not seem right that these six other young men who had died in dreadful circumstances at the hands of Hauptmann Mackensen should still be lying in unmarked graves in the former East Germany.

I am delighted to say that I discovered the grave of Private G.H. Thompson of The Green Howards Regiment, (marked as an 'Unbekannter Englischer Soldat', an 'Unknown English Soldier') who died of dysentery a few weeks before Antony, in a civilian cemetery at Wittenberg, some forty miles to the north-east of Kaltenhof where Antony passed away. It is perfectly possible that Antony would have known him, marched alongside him and mourned his death. The resting place of Private Thompson, among a row of named German soldiers, has now been graced with a proper headstone and was rededicated in 2017 during a military service that I attended with some friends. The army was represented by the officiating padre, an officer from his regimental association and the British Military Attache to

Berlin. Sadly, I could find no living relatives to join us at the service, but at least we have returned his name to him and Private Thompson will not be forgotten again.

That leaves just five to go. Their names are:

Private P.A. Baldwin of The Queen's Own West Kent Regiment.

Private A. Cheshire of the Middlesex Regiment.

Craftsman J.C. Torrance of the Corps of Royal Electrical and Mechanical Engineers.

Private M. Jagger of the Royal Ordnance Service Corps.

Private E. Walker of the Durham Light Infantry Regiment.

I intend to find each one of them and to salute them, as I saluted Antony.

Commander Steve Foster, Royal Navy (retired). Hampshire. May 2018.

ACKNOWLEDGEMENTS

My grateful thanks go to the following people and organisations:

First and foremost, Barbara Willoughby-Thomas, the niece of Antony Coulthard. Without her eager co-operation, her dedicated research into family history, and the time, commitment and love that she gave to the search for Antony's grave, this book would not have been possible. Whenever I doubted that we would succeed, it was Barbara who kept me going.

The author Andrew Robinson, nephew of Antony, who kindly allowed me to see family documents without which the grave would never have been found. I much appreciate his support throughout the writing of this book and his trust in me to tell the story of his remarkable uncle.

My sister Margaret and her son Jonathan for contributing their memories of Fred Foster.

Jonathan Kydd, son of the actor Sam Kydd, for his enthusiasm and his kind permission to quote from his father's book *For You The War Is Over* (Futura Publications 1974 – available via Amazon).

The present day Intelligence Corps at Chicksands. Without the help of the staff at Corps HQ and the staff of Templer Company, much of the story would not have been uncovered. Also, for their subsequent staging of the rededication of Antony's grave. I would particularly like to mention: Colonel (Retired) Jon Murray OBE, Padre Clive Larrett, the late Major (Retired) Alan Edwards, the Corps historian and WO1 (RSM) David Thomas.

Hania and Pavel Bukowski and Michal Targowski, our expert guides at the site of Stalag XXA in Torun, Poland.

Doctor Rolf Meyer and Herr Olli Eicke, our advisers and guides in the area around Kaltendorf, Lower Saxony, Germany and who have so kindly continued to help in the search for the graves of the remaining 'unknown soldiers'.

Herr Hermann Apitz who, as a boy, witnessed the death of Antony Coulthard and whose statement was crucial to the eventual recognition of the grave.

Nicola Nash from the Joint Casualty and Compassionate Centre of the Ministry of Defence who accepted my evidence on the whereabouts of the grave and who subsequently masterminded the rededication service.

The National Archives at Kew and The Imperial War Museum, London, without whose records the final part of the story could not have been written.

Everyone at Mirror Books for offering me the opportunity to bring this story to a wider public: Paula Scott, Jo Sollis, Julie Adams, George Robarts, Simon Flavin and Melanie Sambells.

My wife Christine for putting up with me during the years when I was totally immersed in the research for this story – and for pretending that she wasn't completely fed up with it.

Last but not least, Alan Clark, my co-author. A truly gifted writer who, through his talents, has brought the story in the suitcase back to life and, in the process, has become my friend and confidant. Thanks Alan.

Also by Mirror Books

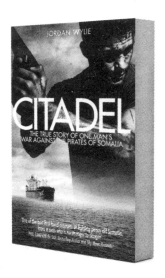

Citadel
Jordan Wylie with Alan Clark

An inspirational true story of danger, adventure and triumph over adversity.

Jordan Wylie, a young man from a tough area of Blackpool where kids like him often go off the rails, opted for life in the army. He saw service in Iraq and learned to cope with the horrors he'd witnessed, then suffered an injury that blocked any chance of climbing up the military ladder.

But an old army colleague suggested he join a security team on a tanker in Yemen. Ex-servicemen were offered dazzling salaries and 'James Bond' lifestyles between jobs protecting super-tankers. However, the price they paid was a life of claustrophobia and isolation along with the ever-present possibility of death skimming towards them across the vast, lonely blue sea. In Citadel, Jordan writes the first account of these dangerous years from someone 'at the front'. A young soldier from the backstreets of Blackpool, determined to make the most of his life, but unsure of the way forward. He found his answers in the perilous waters of 'Pirate Alley'.

Mirror Books

Also by Mirror Books

Falling Through Fire
Clifford Thompson

The true story of a London firefighter, now journalist, and his involvement in domestic and high-profile disasters across 25 years.

One incident, early in his career, had a profound effect on him that he carries to this day.

In a frank and honest way he recounts his personal experience of the 1988 Clapham train crash, the 1993 bombing of New York's World Trade Centre and the aftermath of the King's Cross fire.

Clifford describes the trauma that firefighters deal with on a daily basis – and reveals that despite facing many horrific situations and experiencing major disasters, he cannot escape the haunting memory of a three-year-old boy dying in his arms after a house fire just days before Christmas.

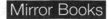

Also by Mirror Books

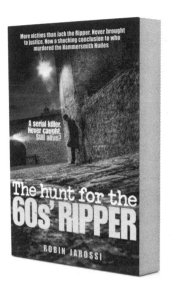

The Hunt for the 60s Ripper
Robin Jarossi

While 60s London was being hailed as the world's most fashionably vibrant capital, a darker, more terrifying reality was unfolding on the streets. During the early hours a serial killer was stalking prostitutes then dumping their naked bodies. When London was famed for its music, groundbreaking movies and Carnaby Street vibe, the reality included a huge street prostitution scene, a violent world that filled the magistrate's courts.

Seven, possibly eight, women fell victim – making this killer more prolific than Jack the Ripper, 77 years previously. His grim spree sparked the biggest police manhunt in history. But why did such a massive hunt fail? And why has such a traumatic case been largely forgotten today?

With shocking conclusions, one detective makes an astonishing new claim. Including secret police papers, crime reconstructions, links to figures from the vicious world of the Kray twins and the Profumo Affair, this case exposes the depraved underbelly of British society in the Swinging Sixties. An evocative and thought-provoking reinvestigation into perhaps the most shocking unsolved mass murder in modern British history.

Mirror Books

Also by Mirror Books

Unrest
Jesper Stein

European best-selling author Jesper Stein's award-winning debut thriller, Unrest, introduces Danish DCI Axel Stein.

A body is found in a cemetery in the Norrebro area of Copenhagen, just yards from a heavily guarded 'youth house' that is being forcibly cleared by police. Dressed in dark camouflage clothes and propped against a wall, how is anyone murdered and left in the open with so many police on site.
Unless the killer was one of them..?

Stein is assigned the case which quickly becomes more complicated and more personal than he could ever have imagined…

Released for the first time in English, this immensely popular and exciting set of best-selling books kicks off with a dramatic and fast-paced thriller.

"Jesper Stein writes about a Copenhagen that's both full of change yet always the same, where the human condition must be constantly re-evaluated. It's harsh, dark, yet with a warm, beating heart at its core." – LARS KEPLER

Mirror Books